THE ROLE OF INFORMATION PROFESSIONALS IN THE KNOWLEDGE ECONOMY

Chandos Information Professional Series

Series Editor: Ruth Rikowski

(email: Rikowskigr@aol.com)

Chandos' new series of books is aimed at the busy information professional. They have been specially commissioned to provide the reader with an authoritative view of current thinking. They are designed to provide easy-to-read and (most importantly) practical coverage of topics that are of interest to librarians and other information professionals. If you would like a full listing of current and forthcoming titles, please visit www.chandospublishing.com.

New authors: We are always pleased to receive ideas for new titles; if you would like to write a book for Chandos, please contact Dr Glyn Jones on g.jones.2@elsevier.com or telephone +44 (0) 1865 843000.

THE ROLE OF INFORMATION PROFESSIONALS IN THE KNOWLEDGE ECONOMY

Skills, Profile and a Model for Supporting Scientific Production and Communication

JAVIER TARANGO

JUAN D. MACHIN-MASTROMATTEO

ELSEVIER

CP
CHANDOS
PUBLISHING
An imprint of Elsevier • elsevier.com

Chandos Publishing is an imprint of Elsevier
50 Hampshire Street, 5th Floor, Cambridge, MA 02139, United States
The Boulevard, Langford Lane, Kidlington, OX5 1GB, United Kingdom

British Library Cataloguing-in-Publication Data
A catalogue record for this book is available from the British Library

Library of Congress Cataloging-in-Publication Data
A catalog record for this book is available from the Library of Congress

ISBN: 978-0-12-811222-9 (print)
ISBN: 978-0-12-811223-6 (online)

For information on all Chandos Publishing publications
visit our website at https://www.elsevier.com/books-and-journals

Publisher: Glyn Jones
Acquisition Editor: Glyn Jones
Editorial Project Manager: Thomas Van Der Ploeg
Production Project Manager: Debasish Ghosh
Designer: Mark Rogers

Typeset by MPS Limited, Chennai, India

CONTENTS

BIOGRAPHIES

Javier Tarango is a full-time professor and researcher at the Universidad Autónoma de Chihuahua (UACH) in Mexico and is a member of the National Researchers System. He holds a PhD in Education (UACH), a Master's degree in Information Science (Universidad de Guanajuato, Mexico), a Master's degree in Organisational Development (Universidad de Monterrey, Mexico), and a Bachelor's degree in Pedagogy (UACH). Since 1996, he has been working at the UACH in the Master's and Doctor's Degrees in Education and the Bachelor's Degree in Information Science; and is the leader of the academic body of Information Studies. His lines of research are information literacy and evaluation of scientific production. He has published eight books, 20 book chapters, 38 peer-reviewed and indexed scientific articles, 24 proceedings at length, and 72 papers. He has supervised 27 master's and doctoral theses, has delivered over 100 courses as an instructor, 15 specialized consultancies, and coordinated nine research projects. In addition, he is a peer reviewer for the scientific journals *Cuadernos de Documentación Multimedia*, *E-Ciencias de la Documentación*, *Journal of New Approaches in Educational Research*, *Revista General de Información y Documentación*, *Tecnociencias*, *Revista General de Información*, and *Revista Interamericana de Bibliotecología*; as well as six academic books (Elsevier).

Juan Daniel Machin-Mastromatteo is a full-time professor and researcher at the Universidad Autónoma de Chihuahua (UACH) in Mexico and is a member of the National Researchers System. He holds a PhD in Information and Communication Science (Tallinn University, Estonia), a Master's degree in Digital Library Learning (Oslo and Akershus University College of Applied Sciences, Norway; Tallinn University; and Parma University, Italy), and a Bachelor's degree in Library Science (Universidad Central de Venezuela). He has more than 10 years of work experience in archives, libraries, higher education, and professional development. He has excelled in different roles, such as as a cataloguer, database developer, reference librarian, instructor, collection developer, designer of library promotion materials and multimedia resources, coordinator of information literacy programs in higher education institutions, scientific production analyst, consultant, and peer reviewer for scientific journals. He has published 23 refereed and indexed articles, three books, six book chapters and has presented papers in 29 international conferences related to his various lines of research: informational literacy, evaluation of scientific production, open access, information architecture, and digital libraries. Machin-Mastromatteo is a permanent editorial board member of the scientific journals *Information Development* (Sage; where, since 2015, he has also written and published the regular column *Developing Latin America*) and *Information and Learning Science* (Emerald). He is a peer reviewer for *Information Development, Information and Learning Science, Journal of Academic Librarianship* (Elsevier), *Scientometrics* (Springer), and *International Journal of Educational Technology in Higher Education* (Springer).

INTRODUCTION

This book redefines the role and skills of information professionals as scientific production and communication managers. It presents tools, products, and resources that are necessary for universities and research institutions (knowledge institutions) to acquire and develop a scientific culture; a key area that defines their international competitiveness. It highlights the importance of information professionals as scientific production and communication managers in such institutions.

This book is ideal for information professionals and students who are interested in scientific production and communication as avenues of endeavor. Researchers, professors, and decision-makers involved in knowledge generation processes will also find useful insights for enabling their institutions and staff to advance in this area and remain competitive in this vital activity of the knowledge economy.

The key features that are analyzed in this book are: the idea that an information professional is the right person to support scientific production and communication; it provides the guidance needed to develop an institutional scientific culture that is capable of producing scientific documents, patents, innovation, and value to society, which are used to measure and evaluate an institutions' competitiveness; it identifies the competencies needed by information professionals with a stake in scientific production and communication; and it redefines the profile of such information professionals and identifies this new skillset as a job opportunity.

Scientific productivity, scientific production, academic production, scientific communication, and scientific dissemination are often unified under the umbrella term "scholarly communication," however these terms are defined as separate but related entities in this book. Given this distinction, that is explained within, this book is part of the scientific production, academic production, and scientific communication belonging to the authors and their institutions of affiliation. It represents a portion of our scientific production, as its writing involved various rounds of brainstorming, revision, and rewriting; after that, the publisher as well as some experts reviewed its content in order to ensure it had academic and scientific rigor, value, and quality. It is an academic production, as its contents are derived from both authors' formal training, as well as from the lectures and conferences they have delivered about the topics covered within this book. Such topics are of worldwide academic interest: they are useful for professionals from all disciplines and for decision-makers that coordinate research groups or direct knowledge institutions and wish to know how to strengthen, measure, or promote research in their institutions. This book is also a manifestation of scientific communication, as its contents were conveniently packaged—in a structure we hope is useful for you—and made available to its intended audience by the publisher, and hence we are communicating its scientific contents to you. It takes into consideration other related scientific works, but it is presented in an accessible language, including theoretical perspectives and lessons, which will make it useful for a broader audience.

The book is divided into four chapters. Chapter 1, Scientific Production in the Knowledge Economy and its Influence on the Competitiveness of Universities and Research Institutions, provides insights about the relationship between scientific production and the knowledge economy. This is a topic widely applied to various institutional and social sectors, but it is challenging to implement it efficiently and equitably at a macro level, both from the perspectives of assessing its influence and of measuring its impact. The study of the knowledge economy in relation to scientific production contributes to the identification of competitiveness indicators for knowledge institutions, to understand how research and knowledge generation should be prioritized in such institutions, and to plan strategies for developing this area and remain competitive.

Chapter 2, Conceptualization of Scientific Productivity, Production, Dissemination, and Communication, identifies the importance of knowledge generation processes and the role they play in knowledge institutions. It also defines the main concepts related to scientific research and knowledge generation: scientific productivity, scientific production, academic production, scientific communication, and scientific dissemination. These concepts are classified given their importance in the measurement of knowledge and science. Moreover, the various types of valid scientific products resulting from knowledge generation are defined.

Chapter 3, The New Profile of Information Professionals as Scientific Production and Communication Managers: Identification of Competences, presents the competences that information professionals must develop in their practice within and outside libraries if they work as scientific production and communication agents, which is a new area of opportunity for information professionals. Such competences are relevant for the information professionals that develop activities related to scientific production and communication management in knowledge institutions. It categorizes scientific competences into four basic types: information, linguistic, communication, and digital. It is also proposed that this new profile of information professionals as scientific production and communication managers is based upon another five competences that complement the previous scientific competences: science evaluation; research processes and types; scientific style and writing manuals; databases and information search strategies; and scientific legislation.

Chapter 4, An Academic Model to Support Scientific Production and Communication, proposes a model to support the development of scientific processes in knowledge institutions. This model's objectives, scope, and methodological issues are defined, as it focuses on strengthening the generation of the scientific productivity environment, which will enable the successful generation of scientific production, communication, and dissemination. It explains five organizational structures that are proposed as alternatives to implement this model in knowledge institutions: mutual collaboration, direct supervision, standardization of working processes, standardization of competences and knowledge, and the development of an integral model. The basic services that an institutional department or unit based upon the model proposed are analyzed, these include: information needs diagnostics; searching for information sources; identification of information sources for scientific communication and dissemination; editing and preparing manuscripts for publication; data transcription, preparation, processing, and analysis; translation of scientific documents; information metrics studies; user satisfaction analysis; and training programs. Some concluding remarks are also offered at the end of the book.

CHAPTER 1

Scientific Production in the Knowledge Economy and its Influence on the Competitiveness of Universities and Research Institutions

1.1 INTRODUCTION

It is essential to start this chapter from the main functions of the university, which can be also generally applied to other research institutions. According to Ortega y Gasset (2007), these functions are represented in the following processes: (1) knowledge teaching and learning; (2) research; and (3) extension through scientific communication. Although these correspond to the classical foundations established in the published literature on educational theory, they represent a common thread to recognize that the inclusion of the knowledge economy (KE) idea in higher education and research institutions (knowledge institutions) has resulted in a source of indicators for measuring organizational competitiveness. Whitley (2008) considers that knowledge institutions have tended to mimic business' functional structures and planning processes, incorporating new concepts of measurement, which include competitiveness, quality, and profitability, exceeding an initially epistemic vision.

Conceptually, the KE is based on the production, distribution, and use of information and knowledge (Organization for Economic Co-operation & Development [OECD], 1996), thereby creating epistemic networks, whose intense relationships generate new knowledge and determine the socioeconomic position of both individuals and organizations (Clarke, 2001). Although knowledge often has various manifestations, the most common is its transmission through the processes of education and training of human resources. This chapter examines knowledge generation, implementation, and communication (through

The Role of Information Professionals in the Knowledge Economy
DOI: http://dx.doi.org/10.1016/B978-0-12-811222-9.00001-7

research processes), especially in relation to its transfer as a contribution for innovation and scientific communication.

According to Avilés-Fabila (2009), the traditional core functions of universities are seen as normal and, therefore, are basic and elemental. Although knowledge generation, both in individuals and institutions, is well recognized as a core function that is related to the KE, it seems that its implications represent a different function. Knowledge generation has been added to the traditionally recognized functions used for measuring the competitiveness of knowledge institutions, but it is now affected by the notion of profitability, beyond an academic prestige that is based on theoretical idealisms; however, such a situation does not imply dismissing the social function of knowledge.

The core function of knowledge generation, implementation, and communication as an indicator of scientific production demands the fulfilment of two fundamental issues: (1) identifying the stakeholders that are responsible for such processes; and (2) defining the quality of knowledge. Each issue has its own definitions and characteristics, which must be accurately understood in order to discuss their connections with the following content.

Regarding knowledge stakeholders, we can identify many of them: students, thesis candidates, professors and researchers, institutional authorities, members of society, business people, as well as the professors and researchers from other institutions. Professors and researchers are mainly seen as having the largest leadership responsibility concerning the generation of knowledge that can contribute directly to the KE. The generation of knowledge under such leadership should happen robustly in their institutions, through scientific communication conducted only using certified contents and formats that are derived from research (Whitley, 2008). If knowledge institutions play an important role in the globalization of knowledge, professors and researchers are better able to apply knowledge to solve problems, thus favoring institutional, regional, and national growth (Deiaco, Hughs, & McKelvery, 2012). This is why professors and researchers are favored as an actor in scientific communication processes. However, it is also necessary to assess and reassess the role of the information professional as an intermediary; which is appropriately trained for aiding in these processes, so they can take place effectively.

Regarding the quality of the knowledge generated and formally communicated (explicit), knowledge institutions must appropriately identify their lines of research, basing them on collective goals rather than on individual ones. They must recognize, in a precise way, the functions of scientific research and communication within the work activities of professors and researchers, which go beyond mere teaching processes. The inclusion of the KE as part of knowledge institutions' growth, will undoubtedly demand considering certain measurement mechanisms that can define if the scientific production being developed is actually contributing to institutional goals, if the performance of each actor involved is substantial (both regarding quality and quantity) and to what extent, if the products being generated are having an impact on the generation of new knowledge through cooperation with other highly recognized persons and institutions, which are identified as scientific communities.

The participation of professors and researchers with the scientific knowledge generated, takes place as a relationship of interdependence that is symbiotic, if either of them is absent, then it is impossible to contribute to the generation of a KE (Eikeland, 2013). Such dependence encourages the emergence of scientific communities that will allow a greater capacity for innovation, which is understood as those research processes that meet society's needs in general. These communities must be able to produce scientific knowledge, their results become public science when their contributions are accepted for communication through information sources of high validity and recognition, and then by generating knowledge transmission mechanisms for industry and society. Such an intellectual function that is described here is linked with knowledge transfer through formal scientific production and communication, which are judged as elements of measurable knowledge, due to their objectivity and contribution to the KE. Núñez-Guerrero and Rodríguez-Monroy (2014) are more specific in classifying the knowledge formally generated into four types: (1) scientific-technical knowledge, which is intrinsically contained in the individuals, as part of the social capital; (2) research knowledge, which involves the application of research techniques and the scientific method to build it; (3) interdisciplinary research groups' knowledge, which is the sum of individual and collective experiences that are used to generate holistic knowledge; and (4) knowledge regarding the management of tangible resources, which involves transfer and communication through various media.

To sum up, the delimitation of the approach presented starts from identifying the social role of knowledge institutions through extension processes that are used in formal scientific communication, by considering various knowledge objects that are derived from research, whose conditions are characterized by their quality. It is highly strategic to value professors and researchers as key players for knowledge transmission and communication processes to take place, which makes it possible to build the intellectual and social capital that the KE demands.

1.2 KNOWLEDGE'S INFLUENCE IN EDUCATION AND RESEARCH DEVELOPMENT

The globalization of the KE includes broad aspects that are supposed to impact society in general. In this chapter, the application of the KE's principles is restricted in particular to knowledge institutions, with a specific focus on the issues that are related to scientific production and communication. This delimitation was made due to the wide range of approaches available and because of the complexity of measuring the KE's impact in a more holistic manner. Under this perspective, Roberts (2009) attempts to simplify and summarize the different views that could be considered when applying the KE to institutional settings, considering that: (1) the true impact of knowledge in the economy should identify different processes that are based on inputs and outputs; (2) information and communications technologies (ICT) are infrastructure elements that play a key role; (3) knowledge commercialization as capital goods is part of the process involving the conversion of intangible into tangible knowledge; and (4) the proportional development and growth of knowledge workers will represent the competitiveness of their institutions.

For Aragonés and Salgado (2013), the above aspects can be hypothetical and utopian conditions in the case of the educational sector, because they consider that they are typical of the business sector and hence they leave out many social aspects; which should characterize knowledge institutions. A business vision of the KE that loses a sense of sensitivity, can cause various social crises that are not theoretically covered. For example, in the case of migrant populations, there is often a total lack of attention in relation to knowledge-related actions; this is also evident in those sectors that are stagnated regarding their educational attainment levels because of unemployment and low economic and social conditions. There is a tendency to relate the KE exclusively to exact sciences, technology, engineering, and mathematics, leaving aside the humanities and social sciences.

Given its complexity, it is necessary to consider the concept of "knowledge" as a key element of this study, based on the fact that it is an intangible asset and it is literally deposited in the minds of the subjects and that it tends to constantly increase and be modified. Therefore, knowledge is difficult to control, both in its origin and its flow (Psarras, 2006). In order to reach knowledge itself, we require to advance through a differentiated process of three fundamental moments: (1) data: isolated elements or signs; (2) information: data that are appropriately structured in documents of any format; and, (3) knowledge: the use of information to solve practical problems, including the generation of new knowledge. This process is characterized by formally structuring data through information mediums, for their later use and application, allowing to practically reach the objectification of knowledge, so when it becomes a tangible good it is possible to manage it, reuse it, hold it, and transfer it (Vega-Encabo, 2009).

From the objectification of knowledge, the concept of knowledge management (KM) is incorporated. This concept, in the case of knowledge institutions, will represent a key tool for measuring competitiveness, since the data–information–knowledge–information flow is present in an endless cycle. KM is able to influence both the individuals of such organizations as well as those individuals in similar organizations over the world through the forming of scientific communities, participations in academic events such as conferences, symposia, and especially through the use of scientific publications that communicate research findings. Knowledge transfer becomes relevant, as it involves the use and creation of new knowledge in a continuous cycle. For Liebowitz and Suen (2000), this is a cycle characterized by: (1) transforming information into knowledge; (2) identifying and verifying knowledge; and (3) capturing and asserting knowledge.

In relation to the processes of KM and KE, the literature reviewed evidences a strong link of their application with organizations whose performance is measured almost exclusively with the achievement of economic profits from the production or marketing of goods or services; something that is not necessarily applicable to knowledge institutions. For Whitley (2008), the importance of differentiating the concepts of knowledge according to the type of organization, lies in identifying their unique strategic stakeholders, which will determine the knowledge institution's distinguishing characteristics regarding its organizational capabilities and knowledge needs. A knowledge institution aware of the KE would be expected to develop collective capabilities through the acquisition, use, and readiness of human and material resources; and to turn it into a routine for solving problems.

Knowledge institutions tend to apply the general principles of both KM and the KE. However, it is understood that teachers and researchers are the major stakeholders in knowledge-generating activities, they have particular information needs that correspond to their intellectual objectives, which are determined by their individual and group lines of research within a specific scientific field. The configuration and performance of the stakeholders and institutions generate a series of situations that define the ways in which knowledge takes place and how it is turned from intangible into tangible forms. Knowledge becomes tangible through scientific documents that are made public; a process that does not necessarily occur in other productive sectors.

Therefore, knowledge in knowledge institutions could be considered to have different characteristics than in other organizations; it becomes a highly influential element in educational and research processes, which are specific and restricted to a sector of academic and scientific communities. Lopez-Leyva (2014) developed an analysis of the conceptual approaches regarding knowledge in universities, considering that besides being a foundation for research, it is used for the purpose of transforming students. This transformative purpose includes the transfer of contents to develop awareness, define character, increase competences and skills, and fundamentally nurture students' conditions to increase their employability. Knowledge applications as a foundation for research and transforming students represent complex processes that are independent but mutually influence each other.

It must be added to this discussion that the presence of digital media has transformed workflows in relation to knowledge sharing, whose relationship with scientific production, the KE and the flow of information is called "fluid knowledge" (Area-Moreira & Pessoa, 2012). This concept states that much of the knowledge is not localized, nor under the control of knowledge institutions, but it is dispersed in various storage mediums (databases, digital libraries and open access repositories, laboratories, and the Web 2.0). However, the main stakeholders (teachers and researchers with a high level of digital literacy) are free to communicate this knowledge through sources with high-quality standards (scientific articles published in peer-reviewed and indexed journals, books published by prestigious publishers, patents that are registered with government entities capable of recognizing and evaluating innovation, among others). Here we have two fundamental aspects to consider: (1) developing capabilities for identifying and evaluating information sources, and (2) demonstrating a solid scientific culture.

The responsibility of producing and communicating knowledge is systematically attributed to knowledge institutions. These institutions seek to demonstrate their competitiveness in relation to other similar institutions through various indicators. Larner (2015) states that the current ambition regarding knowledge generation lies in the pursuit of internationalization, which causes an "academic diaspora" with the creation of global knowledge networks; thus creating a series of self-organization processes among academics, scientists, and researchers with the aim of producing and managing knowledge. One of the most visible signs of the academic diaspora effect is evident in those published products where the authorship is related to several institutional affiliations. This aspect makes it difficult to clearly define the ownership of a given knowledge and also to justify the need for knowledge-creating stakeholders to follow globalization-related dynamics.

The actions for spreading knowledge correspond to knowledge transfer processes and can be a means for knowledge institutions to expand and diversify (Dickson, 2009). Developing countries have especially sought to bring professors and researchers closer, in order to have them participate in the growth processes of their own institutions, so they can produce better results through globalization and KE indicators; e.g., through student exchange initiatives and the internationalization of academic programs. Both examples may not contribute directly to scientific production, but they do contribute to the training of future researchers; in turn, the main indicators are those related to the development of explicit knowledge (Boyle, McDonnell, Mitchell, & Nicholas, 2012). Explicit knowledge is of special value for defining competitiveness levels, because it is the formal way of communicating science.

According to the World Bank (2003), learning becomes knowledge both in the short and the long term, but the second is more desirable, since the growth of the human capital in knowledge institutions is determined by the perishability of knowledge (i.e., knowledge that becomes obsolete) as a source capable of critically achieving the economic and social growth of institutions and countries. Knowledge is a key element for development and growth, but should be linked to other aspects such as the provision of technological resources and the access to scientific information sources. These aspects must be present in governmental priorities, as teachers and researchers may not have personal access to those resources and, therefore, a lack of access may prevent them from working on innovation-related issues.

Knowledge can change people and institutions, provided that they have a willingness to change. Meza-Rodriguez (2010) presents some elements that knowledge institutions can take into consideration for demonstrating change: (1) the ability for adapting to current environments through information assimilation, the generation of innovations and habits of being continuously up to date; (2) the presence and influence of national innovation assessment systems, which according to the definition of national scientific policies, can systematically push (or inhibit) the development of research processes; and (3) the relationship between knowledge institutions with ICT. Compliance with these elements will be reflected in the influence that knowledge institutions have over education, economy, science, technology, and innovation; as well as in generating new information infrastructures and the ability to establish relationships between scientific entities.

As was previously discussed in this chapter, knowledge institutions must accurately identify their mission, which must have gained other perspectives in recent years. In fighting for their competitiveness in the KE, knowledge institutions also face many dangers, since knowledge—by becoming a tangible good—becomes a production factor that is governed by traditional market forces. Consequently, it is currently essential to develop mechanisms that are similar to those of lucrative businesses regarding the way they participate in globalization. This could lead professors and researchers to lose the social sense embedded in the role of education and of academic commitment (Jonsson, Baraldi, Larsson, Forsberg, & Severinsson, 2015); as they are forced to comply with a knowledge production that adopts industrial-corporate values, which create expectations of total efficiency and mass production. Moreover, this situation puts those institutions or countries with fewer economic resources at a disadvantage, since the access to the KE also demands solid infrastructures (physical, human, informational, and technological). This phenomenon is called "academic capitalism." Slaughter and Rhoades (2009), in their book *Academic Capitalism and the New Economy*, indicate that academic institutions have focused on knowledge as a public good, capitalizing it in activities oriented at obtaining tangible profits, thus the activities they currently undertake are related to the development, marketing, and sales of research products, educational services, and the consumption of goods from the private market.

The new educational services that are demanded by the KE have generated new forms of work that are related alternative ways of social interaction through knowledge networks, where knowledge creation and dissemination must take place; this situation has redefined the work activities of professors and researchers. For Slaughter and Leslie (2001), these stakeholders need to expand their intellectual capital conditions to various competitive environments that are beyond the academic ones. Even in academic capitalism, the development of independent functions is complementary to their common academic activities, so they become entrepreneurs subsidized by the state and must adapt to other environments that are different from their own.

For Dang and Umemoto (2009), with respect to the KE in knowledge institutions, the ideal is to develop human capital under a knowledge-as-capability vision, where the skills needed to act are identified, by changing routine actions and research roles of professors and researchers. According to these authors, this approach is the most convenient, over other KE-based proposals such as knowledge as goods or knowledge as a means for obtaining relationships, but these other two perspectives may result from the first. Other views suggest that the mere development of knowledge-as-capability has various constraints in relation to organizational learning, although it can cause institutional improvements in specific aspects (selection of students, teaching processes, administrative, research processes of teachers and researchers, and intellectual property processes), it is not a significant reflection of a country's conditions (Cantwell, Kauppinen, & Slaughter, 2014).

Concerns about academic capitalism in the KE and scientific production lie in the excessive materialism that usually happens within knowledge institutions. The basis of the profitability in knowledge institutions regarding their contributions to development (based on regulatory approaches, of facts and policies) and knowledge lie in the production of scientific tangibles (Arocena, Göransson, & Sutz, 2015). Therefore, it is difficult to prove a direct return, but it is indeed possible to measure competitiveness from the perspective of scientific production, which usually counts the number of products published in scientific information sources that are recognized by scientific communities because of their high value and quality.

1.3 THE CREATION, ADAPTATION, DISSEMINATION, AND DEPRECIATION OF SCIENTIFIC KNOWLEDGE

According to the World Bank's (2007) extensive studies on alternatives for building strategies for the KE, research conducted within knowledge institutions has played a crucial role in industrialized countries, which demonstrates the importance of knowledge generation and its influence on the development of institutions and countries. However, this does not apply in developing countries, where universities have a high and almost exclusive focus on academic training processes (specifically teaching); which under the perception of university managers and administrators it seems to exclude knowledge generation and management processes and they especially dismiss research activities by labeling them as nonpriority.

It is therefore necessary to prevent higher education institutions in developing countries from primarily focusing their activities in teaching processes (as this issue is not present in research centers); because if they do, they will generate a number of limitations considering the KE's conditions. Such a scenario would result in higher education institutions that perform instructional transfer activities as their main and only functions rather than also including knowledge creation activities. These would be institutions without research bases and experiences and hence they will not generate enough indicators to be deemed as competent institutions if their scientific production is evaluated. In relation to universities' mission, the mere transfer of knowledge through teaching processes will cover only one possible aspect; therefore, limiting their operation to teaching will alienate higher education institutions from the KE and will keep them far from what their mission and vision should be nowadays. The main problem is that scientific production evaluation and measurement work in the same manner in both developed and developing countries. In the latter case, the development of technological universities has been a solution for contributing to the KE. These institutions contribute to economic development, as they seek to commercialize knowledge through projects, developing industrial property and innovation initiatives directly with the labor market; so this knowledge is not necessarily generated for the development of the institutional intellectual capital.

When considering scientific production as one of the major contributions that knowledge institutions make to the KE, it is important to reiterate their new vision and role in the creation and management of scientific and technical knowledge. Rodríguez-Castellanos, Araujo-de-la-Mata, and Urrutia-Gutierrez (2001) recognize that today's society is based on knowledge, so knowledge institutions are the key elements within innovation systems; and both society and governments push the importance that research has for the economic development of any country.

When recognizing the new role of knowledge institutions for contributing to the KE through scientific production, authors like Bricall (2000) consider that the following aspects are currently demanded: (1) a society that is increasingly informed and linked to activities related to the generation and dissemination of new knowledge; (2) an increasing internationalization of research processes in collaborative networks between professors, researchers, and institutions, as well as the participation of scientific communication media; (3) constant demonstrations of broader scientific multidisciplinarity regarding the themes of the knowledge generated; and (4) recognition of the scientific production of knowledge institutions as a factor of their competitiveness.

From the prioritization of scientific production as a form of knowledge objectification, knowledge institutions' increase in competitiveness indicators and their contributions to the globalized KE, it is important to analyze the knowledge development cycle. The cycle proposed by Bath (2000) identifies its phases in a spiral that consists of four subprocesses: (1) knowledge creation; (2) knowledge adoption; (3) knowledge distribution; and (4) knowledge review; the latter subprocess can also be related to the depreciation of the knowledge's contents. These threads are described below under the various visions contained in the literature reviewed.

Scientific production as a process begins with knowledge creation, which may have two specific origins: (1) knowledge-based on experience, and (2) research-based knowledge. Although these origins are not mutually exclusive, for the purposes of this chapter we will focus on the latter, as it is the knowledge that is considered scientific. Such knowledge becomes public through formal models of scientific communication and it is the easiest to identify as a measurable competitiveness indicator for professors, researchers, institutions, scientific disciplines, and even countries. KE's measurement processes cannot work by taking as an exclusive reference the knowledge arising or spread through scientific dissemination publications of low value, instead, it must primarily consider those scientific publications that have strict peer review processes and hence are recognized by the scientific communities.

Informal scientific production includes the intellectual creations of professors and researchers that are never published or remain as manuscripts but that somehow influence the academic processes of teaching. However, such production does not qualify as an indicator, because it does not involve planning nor control in terms of its quantity, quality, or disciplinary level of specialization. Nor does it imply a collective formal planning (just an individual one at the most), that would allow gathering enough evidence to apply any indicator to measure the impact of such informal production. Therefore, it is complex to consider its characteristics, especially because of the low level of visibility they can achieve among other academics and scientists, beyond the creator of such informal knowledge.

Informal scientific production can hardly demonstrate its influence on the processes of globalization, the creation of measurable knowledge, and the KE. However, it should be acknowledged that it might generate diverse ideas with the potential of leading to the creation of formal knowledge. The purposes of creating scientific knowledge from research are to record the main findings and follow a highly structured process that ends with scientific communication (Alston, Craig, & Pardey, 1998). For Gil and Carrillo (2013), knowledge creation processes allow acquiring new knowledge or updating the knowledge already available, thereby achieving a substantial and even adaptive growth regarding the changing needs experienced by anyone who develops research processes.

In addition to the research processes (scientific experimentation in any form), it is necessary to generate a knowledge adaptation or adoption process, which can be based on harnessing scientific information sources that are generated by other researchers in various institutions, which are the prime materials for the creation of new knowledge and represent the frontiers of knowledge until the creation of new knowledge. Regularly, this step in the knowledge cycle starts from consulting external sources and combining them with the researchers' own scientific experiences, while taking into account various characteristics of scientific rigor for both the knowledge used and the knowledge generated, such as the clarity of the findings, the scope of content, and the knowledge soundness (Bath, 2000; Rodríguez-Castellanos et al., 2001).

According to the United Nations Environment Programme (UNEP, 2016), the knowledge adaptation processes are complex to conduct, given that they start from the synthesis of previously published scientific information, the identification of knowledge gaps in a given discipline, the use of a specific methodology, the implementation of strategies to develop products from the knowledge created, and communicating the resulting products. Usually, this is not the work of only one person, but of collaborative teams. We consider important the inclusion of another concept, known as "prosumption" (production by consumers), which involves the production of a new information and knowledge good from the consumption of other information and knowledge goods by new stakeholders in scientific production and communication, apart from the traditional ones, such as professors, researchers, institutions, and cultural industries

(García-Ruiz, Ramírez-García, & Rodríguez-Rosell, 2014; Ritzer & Jurgenson, 2010).

KM processes both in companies and knowledge institutions, once the knowledge has been assimilated, the next step followed corresponds to knowledge distribution or dissemination with the purpose of sharing it with the members of a particular community. In the case of knowledge institutions, knowledge sharing can happen when professors disclose their scientific or methodological findings to their groups of students or at professional conferences at a national, regional, or international level. However, in order to have an effect measurable according to the KE, knowledge sharing happens through explicit transmission processes in formal science communication media, which have different visibility variables that depend on several aspects, among others: (1) the language in which they were published; (2) the sources' own capabilities of dissemination depending on their range of influence; (3) the broadness of the scientific communities in a given field; and (4) the type of source that was published (Aguado-López & Rogel-Salazar, 2006; Terra, 2007).

In any organization, KM demands knowledge dissemination or diffusion and this is associated with knowledge sharing processes through various interactive activities ranging from workshops, conferences, or any informal activities (Tsui, Chapman, Schnirer, & Stewart, 2006). Darr, Argote, and Epple (1995) consider that the sharing processes performed by researchers imply the selective transfer of contents to certain consumers. Paulin and Suneson (2012) state that knowledge is the same in the different types of organization, so they propose a series of general conditions to ensure that the transfer is effective and it works regardless of the type of organization: (1) define exactly the individuals or communities to which the generated knowledge can be shared; (2) the knowledge shared must contribute to the training of human capital; (3) the interactions and products used for knowledge sharing can be diverse; and (4) the contents must have practical applications and contribute to the generation of new knowledge.

The last phase of the knowledge cycle focuses on reviewing it, it is considered that KM has become a dynamic system of quasiautonomous knowledge production and application that at this phase requires systematic monitoring (Rodríguez-Castellanos et al., 2001). Such a phase allows to evaluate it, by considering including knowledge renewal, its applicability, and its performance; as knowledge has become a public good and it is considered that its constant use will generate new knowledge, thereby avoiding it from being lost.

It should be noted that scientific information could fall into a state of systematic lack of use, because it can experience a natural process of obsolescence, mainly caused by the emergence of new knowledge. It should be taken into consideration that although knowledge institutions generate enormous amounts of knowledge, it is only possible to evaluate the timeliness of a given knowledge if it became explicit, meaning that it had to be registered and formally communicated through scientific media. Therefore, implicit knowledge is forgotten or ignored because it is unknown or it was not surrounded by favorable conditions, which prevents the development of formal management processes that can influence the knowledge institution where such knowledge was created, as well as other institutions.

Generally, it is possible to learn or accumulate knowledge, but in a certain point in time it should be "unlearned" or simply not used anymore, because it reached a state of devaluation (Grubler & Nemet, 2013). In the infometrics field, such a process is known as obsolescence level, a value which indicates that the greater the scientific growth in a given field, the greater and faster this loss of value can occur. Obsolescence conditions may vary depending on the scientific discipline. In some sciences a loss of value ranging from 40% to 100% can happen in one year (computer science, biochemistry, cancer studies); while in other disciplines, documents' lifespans are higher (social sciences and humanities).

The value of learning undergoes a similar process of depreciation, in this case the main factor is the excess of transferred knowledge and consequently this rapid growth of a given discipline influences the high rate at which its usefulness is lost (Darr et al., 1995). Metaphorically, knowledge depreciation is a kind of erosion that stored knowledge suffers. It is hence complicated to obtain an accurate representation of the total production of accumulated knowledge, since much of it ceases to be useful, but the net results of such depreciation can be predicted by analyzing the knowledge productivity curves (Boone, Ganeshan, & Hicks, 2008).

Given the high costs associated with maintaining adequate standards of scientific production and communication in any organization, their related strategies must change (substantially so in the developing countries) toward achieving benefits in the longer term, resulting in a need for change regarding the roles played by professors and researchers. Such strategies would imply the following aspects: (1) learning and knowledge use should become more collaborative, by establishing professional and organizational learning networks among knowledge institutions; (2) given the strong investment that knowledge generation demands, new ways to harness and apply it must be developed; (3) create institutional incentives for ensuring an efficient use of both the existing knowledge as well as the newly created; (4) fulfill the need of educating people in creating a culture of creating, sharing, communicating, and using knowledge; (5) create a dynamic information infrastructure to facilitate the effective communication, dissemination, and processing of information; and (6) apply mechanisms to strengthen innovation in the institutions that can promote the global growth of knowledge, respond to local needs, and create new technologies (World Bank, 2003).

The above-listed aspects represent the fundamental basis for achieving a combination among the elements of academic knowledge and their relation to research and development. For Svare (2016), the processes of joint collaboration among knowledge institutions with companies have not been entirely satisfactory, since the sale of innovation projects to businesses by academic and scientific communities have not reached a high enough level. However, we believe that the development of productive projects could be the ideal way to achieve the profitability indicators in knowledge institutions.

According to Olsen (2015), knowledge institutions have failed to create a strengthened enough environment to enter the KE through research, because there is no culture of knowledge, such a culture is difficult to develop only through training, instead it demands specialized human resources in terms of knowledge generation processes; but many scholars do not have such a profile and they will hardly acquire it or develop it. Generally, current universities have many weaknesses that prevent them from being competitive in research, scientific production, and scientific communication and thus are not capable of entering the globalized KE. Ideally, for such a thing to happen, Meza-Rodriguez (2010) identified the following needs that must be covered, as they can help in generating enough evidence to measure the KE variables: (1) to have a sufficient ICT and information infrastructure; (2) to have qualified education and human resources (with graduate degrees completed and a proven scientific culture); (3) the availability of dynamic innovation systems; (4) to generate sufficient data for encouraging research and development; and (5) to develop activities related to the production, distribution, and use of knowledge, as well as having the appropriate information on knowledge products.

It is essential for knowledge institutions to complete the processes that knowledge follows. Bueno-Campos (2003) provides a benchmark that allows knowledge institutions to truly contribute to the KE through scientific production, by demonstrating their social and financial performance through proper management of their intellectual capital, which includes their intellectual and intangible assets. The key elements for achieving globalization-related objectives in terms of knowledge generation, are based on the creation of a knowledge system with three pillars: research, development, and innovation. The structure of such a system should consist of the following interrelated elements: (1) a scientific system (universities, public research organizations, and agencies for transferring research findings); (2) a public-institutional system (national public science and technology organizations, nongovernmental institutions related to knowledge generation); (3) a public-technological system (scientific and technological parks and museums, technological centers and institutes, and business innovation centers); and (4) a productive system (relationships with companies).

Knowledge systems integrate the main individuals and objects that promote the emergence, development, and updating of scientific production processes. Their main purposes will be reflected in the competitiveness of researchers, knowledge institutions, and scientific disciplines. Knowledge systems allow measuring the indicators related to intellectual and social capital, and the presence of such indicators is a response to the demands of the globalized KE.

1.4 INTELLECTUAL CAPITAL AND SOCIAL CAPITAL: FUNDAMENTAL ELEMENTS IN THE GLOBALIZED KNOWLEDGE ECONOMY

Scientific production will not be possible in those knowledge institutions without the key elements of scientific work expertise and experience. These elements are managed by the people who become basic elements for achieving the processes of the globalized KE. Even so, although some people may be irreplaceable, it is important to have an updated infrastructure and strong relationships with other environments. People and their own knowledge are inseparable assets, but both should be developed in a balanced way. A person without knowledge or a set of information that is not turned into a person's knowledge are unnecessary for the purposes of the KE and scientific production. Therefore knowledge subjects and knowledge objects must be properly combined to become intellectual and social capital under different forms and circumstances.

Brooking (1997) defines intellectual capital as those assets that are centered on the individual, such as: collective expertise, creative ability, problem-solving capabilities, and leadership. Several authors have conceptually defined intellectual capital's components and have applied them to different experiences (Bueno-Campos, 2003; Ramírez-Córcoles, Santos-Peñalver, & Tejeda, 2011; Roos, Bainbridge, & Jacobsen, 2001; Sánchez-Medina, Melián-González, & Hormiga-Pérez, 2007; Todericiua & Serbana, 2015). The contribution of these authors can be summarized as follows:

1. *Human capital.* Conformed by the people who become the potential sources of innovation from where ideas emerge and strategies are defined. This type accumulates: competences, attitudes, and intellectual agility. Human capital, for the purposes of this book, is specifically related to professors and researchers who have acquired knowledge mainly through formal training and they work preponderantly in knowledge institutions. Professors and researchers are main stakeholders in scientific production processes, thus measuring human capital includes weighting the number of full-time researchers and their qualifications; as well as recording and counting the research-related awards, recognitions, and incentives they have received; and their participation in human resources training to foster new researchers.
2. *Organizational or structural capital.* This is the knowledge that organizations have been able to internalize and that remains throughout their structure, processes, and culture. It is important to relate the organizational or structural capital with scientific production, because no professor or researcher conducts research processes independently without belonging to an organizational structure and culture. Published scientific products require researchers to have an institutional affiliation, and these are valued according to an institution's prestige and scientific recognition. Organizational or structural capital includes items such as the information resources and digital databases available through their libraries, the accumulated information over primary and secondary empirical data, and the basic infrastructure of an intangible nature.
3. *Relational capital.* Since organizations are not isolated systems, their interactions with other systems become a valuable asset, especially when other organizations have an adequate conception on a particular institution. Knowledge institutions, through their professors and researchers, are more strengthened regarding their relational capital if they have cooperation ties with similar institutions. Relational capital also includes the relationships in the interior of the institutions

through the activities of the various individuals and departments in them, which can generate research groups that encourage collegial work. In particular, relational capital includes: participation in scientific meetings (such as conferences and symposia), membership in scientific societies, and collaboration with other institutions (different to their own) through research groups.

Bueno-Campos (2003) specifies that the tangible results from the three forms of intellectual capital as a consequence of research processes can be considered as: (1) scientific production (publication of books and articles in scientific publications, patent registration, and other intellectual property instruments; the implementation of research projects; and presentations and lectures at conferences); (2) social assessment of the institution through the dissemination of research findings; and (3) an increase of the knowledge institutions' intellectual capital.

To be consistent with the KE's requirements, it is necessary to identify the intellectual capital measuring processes that lead to the definition of the knowledge institutions' competitiveness parameters. Various guidelines for measuring intellectual capital in universities have been proposed: the identification of their resources (level of potential), activities (knowledge creation and renewal processes), and results in terms of knowledge quality levels (performance level) (Fazlagic, 2007; Sánchez, 2006; Secundo, Margherita, Elia, & Passiante, 2010). Intellectual capital measurement refers to the quantities of outputs, as such it includes items such as scientific publications resulting from research, knowledge applications, and the proportion of researchers per institution in relation to the total staff, among others. The measurement of intellectual capital will define any increases regarding the productivity of knowledge-based jobs.

It is important to record intellectual capital in knowledge institutions because it is the most concrete way of identifying the inputs and outputs of knowledge products in each institution, which emerge from scientific and technical research (research results and publications) or through teaching (identification of graduate students that were trained as new researchers and the establishment of productive relationships among scientific communities) (Kucharþíkováa, Tokarþíkováa, & Blaškováa, 2015; Ramírez, Tejeda, & Garduño, 2013). Although knowledge products are often considered intangible assets, it can be stated that scientific communication media have become the main accountability mechanisms of knowledge institutions.

The close relationship between human capital and the KE lies mainly in the clear distinction between the employees who are part of the knowledge production dynamics and those who are not and hence only perform activities of an almost repetitive nature (Díaz-Pérez, 2012). A distinctive factor of human capital, from the management perspective and in relation to the KE, is the conceptual distinction between: (1) values, which include: academic freedom, ethics and research integrity, collegial work, institutional autonomy, intellectual criticism, collective knowledge creation, and open knowledge systems; and (2) value: usefulness magnitude in relation to knowledge production, use of knowledge for promoting progress in society, cultural contributions of local and global importance, actions focused on competitiveness, high ability to transfer knowledge, and the aspects related to the use of ICTs (Abrahams & FitzGerald, 2015; Yu & Zhou, 2015). This distinction is necessary especially in universities, where knowledge production gets a new significance in terms of its measurement, since it usually precedes other values.

In connection with the theory of social capital, Bourdieu (2007) defines it, from a sociological standpoint, as a variable that measures the collaboration between different groups of a collective, obviating the individual opportunities and working from trust, norms, and social interactions. Such social relationships foster the collaborative work of collective action that should lead to the development of different products. Such products resulting from these social relationships can influence decision-making, the management and mobilization of resources, communication, coordination, integration, and conflict resolution.

Various publications have presented a clear classification of the social capital theory (Bourdieu, 2000, 2003, 2007, 2009; Bourdieu, Chamboredon, & Passeron, 1975; Bourdieu & Wacquant, 2005), which is divided into the following items that are related to scientific production in the globalized KE:

1. *Economic capital.* This is the provision of financial resources. While the KE represents an ideal model toward knowledge globalization for competitiveness, it demands the availability of economic resources needed to develop other types of capital (intellectual, structural, relational, social, symbolic, and cultural), and hence it is located over any individual will.
2. *Social capital.* Usually intangible resources based on group membership, relationships, networks of influence, and collaboration. The concept of social relations described by Bourdieu has extensive similarities with the relational capital proposed by Brooking (1997).
3. *Symbolic capital.* A series of intangible properties inherent to individuals, which only exist when they are recognized by others, especially

by those within the same environment. In the case of the KE, this happens when researchers recognize the prestige levels of other researchers who are at an equal or higher level. It is apparent even when researchers refer to the intellectual works of others, e.g., through the citations they use in their scientific publications.

4. *Cultural capital.* This includes the different forms of knowledge, education, and skills, which as a whole give competitive advantages to a person. This type of capital is first acquired from the family by the transmission and acquisition of attitudes, knowledge, traditions, and ways of thinking, which is conceptualized as "habitus" or incorporated cultural capital. The characteristics that conform cultural capital are further reinforced through formal education (known as "field" and corresponding to institutionalized social capital) and it is expected to produce an objectified social capital through cultural goods, represented by scientific publications. The cultural capital proposed by Bourdieu has a broad relationship with the human capital described by Brooking (1997).

The relationship of social capital with knowledge institutions (especially those of a public nature) is reciprocal: the institutions are part of the social capital of their country and the country's social capital was potentially formed by its institutions, through the happening of sociohistorical moments, knowledge building, and the generation of knowledge networks for contributing to new knowledge (Chapela & Jarillo, 2004). It is important to consider that social capital operates from a wealth of scientific information, which makes it possible to focus actions, without forgetting that it is costly and it frequently depends on its constant acquisition (Gordon & Millán, 2004).

Sometimes, collaboration in knowledge networks may reduce the costs of scientific information, provided that knowledge institutions prove to be immersed in the KE. However, collaboration occasionally takes place at a modest extent because of the scientific competition between researchers and institutions (Goudard & Lubrano, 2010). Such levels of competition can occur within a single institution and can originate other individual competition processes, which have a tendency to: (1) make comparisons and claims regarding the number of published products; (2) have coauthored research and writing only with people from other institutions or countries. In addition, it would lead to work strategies characterized by: developing individual activities instead of collective ones, maintaining an obsession for publishing in the top scientific journals, and conditioning scientific production and communication addressing only the requirements of such journals and focusing exclusively on the publication of the products that are most valued by the institutions (for example, giving prominence to scientific articles because of their advantages over other scientific communication types, such as books, book chapters, or theses). The fierce competition can cause scientific production to be conditioned by regulations and requirements (Txapartegui, 2009), rather than being carried out for the true development of a solid social capital.

For both human capital and social capital, any indicator proposed to measure them will require them to demonstrate the level of immersion the institution has in the KE. Although knowledge is an intangible good, Gordon and Millán (2004) propose to identify specific indicators that should be objectified through production results and the scientific communication conducted, thus considering the following measures: (1) individual (personal); (2) according to the level of experience (individual and group); (3) development and implementation of individual strategies; (4) development and implementation of strategies through collaborations; and (5) social capital's level of development at an institutional level. Demonstrating the levels of membership to the KE through the development of human and social capital, according to scientific production, demands introducing a scientific productivity lifecycle model that measures advancements between discrete periods of time (lifecycles' achievements profile) instead of measuring them with continuous time models (by the accumulation of human capital), thus being possible to measure individual, institutional, disciplinary, regional, and national actions (Goudard & Lubrano, 2013).

From any perspective, knowledge has become a scientific endeavor in which social dimensions take precedence over institutional ones. Scientific production is governed by market requirements as well as those of scientific communities, lines of research, knowledge networks or epistemic networks, individual motivations, spatial measures (disciplinary, geographical), or temporal (periods of participation) (Gómez, 2009; Ibarra, 2009; Txapartegui, 2009). It is worth noting three conclusions to consider regarding the aspects mentioned in this chapter, specifically scientific production and the development of human and social capital: (1) the levels of interrelation define the membership conditions for knowledge institutions to be immersed in the KE; (2) scientific knowledge should not only be thought about in relation to professors and researchers, but it must also consider the participation of the general public in the scientific activity, at least in knowing about its current condition (De Donato, 2009); and (3) scientists are not born, although every human being has the capacity to be a scientist, not everyone is an active subject of science, either because of limitations of interests or capabilities (Echeverría, 2009).

REFERENCES

Abrahams, L., & FitzGerald, P. (2015). Would 'good' values yield good 'value'? Positioning higher education in an emerging Knowledge Economy. *Journal of the Knowledge Economy*, *6*(1), 125–137. Available from http://dx.doi.org/10.1007/s13132-012-0116-5.

Aguado-López, E., & Rogel-Salazar, R. (2006). Redalyc: Red de Revistas Científicas de América Latina, el Caribe, España y Portugal: un balance a tres años de camino. In D. Babini, & J. Fraga (Eds.), *Edición Electrónica, Bibliotecas Virtuales y Portales para las Ciencias Sociales en América Latina y el Caribe* (pp. 209–233). Buenos Aires, Argentina: CLACSO. <http://bibliotecavirtual.clacso.org.ar/ar/libros/secret/babini/Aguado%20Lopez%20Salazar.pdf>.

Alston, J., Craig, B., & Pardey, P. (1998). *Dynamics in the creation and depreciation of knowledge, and the returns to research*. Washington, DC, USA: International Food Policy Research Institute. <http://ebrary.ifpri.org/cdm/ref/collection/p15738coll2/id/125676> Accessed 16.08.09.

Aragonés, A., & Salgado, U. (2013). La crisis y la economía del conocimiento en Estados Unidos: Su impacto en la política migratoria. *Norteamérica, 8*(2), 71–104. Available from http://dx.doi.org/10.1016/S1870-3550(13)71774-9.

Area-Moreira, M., & Pessoa, T. (2012). From solid to liquid: New literacies to the cultural changes of Web 2.0. *Comunicar, 19*(38), 13–20.

Arocena, R., Göransson, B., & Sutz, J. (2015). Knowledge policies and universities in developing countries: Inclusive development and the "developmental university". *Technology in Society, 41*, 10–20. Available from http://dx.doi.org/10.1016/j.techsoc.2014.10.004.

Avilés-Fabila, R. (2009). ¿Las funciones sustantivas de la universidad pública son realmente tres? Intertexto con Laura Regil Vargas: Difusión cultural universitaria: Entre el ocaso y el porvenir. *Reencuentro, 56*, 66–69. <http://www.redalyc.org/articulo.oa?id=34011860012> Accessed 16.08.09.

Bath, G. (2000). Organizing knowledge in the knowledge development cycle. *Journal of Knowledge Management, 4*(1), 15–26. Available from http://dx.doi.org/10.1108/13673270010315371.

Boone, T., Ganeshan, R., & Hicks, R. (2008). Learning and knowledge depreciation in professional services. *Management Science, 54*(7), 1231–1236. Available from http://dx.doi.org/10.1287/mnsc.1070.0849.

Bourdieu, P. (2000). *Poder, derecho y clases sociales*. Charleston, SC, USA: CreateSpace Independent Publishing.

Bourdieu, P. (2003). *Los Herederos: los estudiantes y la cultura*. Mexico, D.F., Mexico: Siglo XXI.

Bourdieu, P. (2007). *Capital cultural, escuela y espacio social* (7th ed.) Mexico, D.F., Mexico: Siglo XXI.

Bourdieu, P. (2009). *Homo academicus*. Mexico, D.F., Mexico: Siglo XXI Editores.

Bourdieu, P., & Wacquant, L. (2005). *Una invitación a la sociología reflexiva*. Mexico, D.F., Mexico: Siglo XXI.

Bourdieu, P., Chamboredon, J., & Passeron, J. (1975). *El Oficio del sociólogo*. Mexico, D.F., Mexico: Siglo XXI.

Boyle, B., McDonnell, A., Mitchell, R., & Nicholas, S. (2012). Managing knowledge in internationalizing universities through foreign assignments. *International Journal of Educational Management, 26*(3), 302–312. Available from http://dx.doi.org/10.1108/09513541211213363.

Bricall, J. (2000). *Universidad 2000: Informe sobre la enseñanza superior en España.* Madrid, España: Conferencia de Rectores de las Universidades Españolas. <http://www.ub.edu/web/ub/ca/sites/reforma/pdf/informe_bricall.pdf> Accessed 16.08.09.

Brooking, A. (1997). *El capital intelectual.* Barcelona, España: Paidós.

Bueno-Campos, E. (Ed.), (2003). *Gestión del conocimiento en universidades y organismos públicos de investigación* Madrid, España: Universidad Autónoma de Madrid, Dirección General de Investigación, Consejería de Educación Comunidad de Madrid. <http://www.madrimasd.org/informacionidi/biblioteca/publicacion/doc/16_GestionConocimientoUniversidadesOPIS.pdf> Accessed 16.08.09.

Cantwell, B., Kauppinen, I., & Slaughter, S. (2014). *Academic capitalism in the age of globalization.* New York, USA: Johns Hopkins University Press.

Chapela, M., & Jarillo, E. (2004). El capital social en el futuro de la universidad. *Reencuentro, 40*, 1–13. <http://www.redalyc.org/articulo.oa?id=34004009> Accessed 16.08.09.

Clarke, T. (2001). The knowledge economy. *Education + Training, 43*(4/5), 189–196. Available from http://dx.doi.org/10.1108/00400910110399184.

Dang, D., & Umemoto, K. (2009). Modeling the development toward the knowledge economy: A national capability approach. *Journal of Knowledge Management, 13*(5), 359–372. Available from http://dx.doi.org/10.1108/13673270910988169.

Darr, E., Argote, L., & Epple, D. (1995). The acquisition, transfer, and depreciation of knowledge in service organizations: Productivity in franchises. *Management Science, 41* (11), 1750–1762. Available from http://dx.doi.org/10.1287/mnsc.41.11.1750.

De Donato, X. (2009). La pregunta por los sujetos y la dimensión social de la ciencia. In F. Broncano, & A. Pérez (Eds.), *La ciencia y sus sujetos: ¿Quiénes hacen la ciencia del siglo XXI?* (pp. 181–195). Mexico, D.F., Mexico: Siglo XXI.

Deiaco, E., Hughs, A., & McKelvery, M. (2012). Universities as strategic actors in the knowledge economy. *Cambridge Journal of Economics, 36*(3), 525–541. Available from http://dx.doi.org/10.1093/cje/bes024.

Díaz-Pérez, C. (2012). Tendencias y requerimientos del mercado de trabajo en la economía del conocimiento: Estudio sobre los egresados del CUCEA. *Revista de la Educación Superior, 41*(161), 9–30. <http://publicaciones.anuies.mx/pdfs/revista/Revista161_S1A1ES.pdf> Accessed 16.08.09.

Dickson, T. (2009). Knowledge transfer and the globalisation of higher education. *Journal of Knowledge-Based Innovation in China, 1*(3), 174–184. Available from http://dx.doi.org/10.1108/1756141091099056.

Echeverría, J. (2009). Los sujetos de las ciencias. In F. Broncano, & A. Pérez (Eds.), *La ciencia y sus sujetos: ¿Quiénes hacen la ciencia el siglo XXI?* (pp. 19–26). Mexico, D.F., Mexico: Siglo XXI, (pp. 19–26).

Eikeland, O. (2013). Symbiotic learning systems: Reorganizing and integrating learning efforts and responsibilities between Higher Educational Institutions (HEIs) and work places. *Journal of the Knowledge Economy, 4*(1), 98–118. Available from http://dx.doi.org/10.1007/s13132-012-0123-6.

Fazlagic, A. (2007). Measuring the intellectual capital on a university; Conference on: Trends in the management of human resources in higher education. s.l.: Organisation for Economic Co-operation and Development. <https://www.oecd.org/edu/imhe/35322785.pdf> Accessed 16.08.09.

García-Ruiz, R., Ramírez-García, A., & Rodríguez-Rosell, M. (2014). Educación en alfabetización mediática para una nueva ciudadanía prosumidora. *Comunicar, 22*(43), 15–23. Available from http://dx.doi.org/10.3916/C43-2014-01.

Gil, A., & Carrillo, F. (2013). Knowledge creation in organizations through learning. *Intangible Capital, 9*(3), 730–753. Available from http://dx.doi.org/10.3926/ic.418.

Gómez, A. (2009). La dimensión individual y colectiva de los sujetos de la ciencia. In F. Broncano, & A. Pérez (Eds.), *La ciencia y sus sujetos: ¿Quiénes hacen la ciencia el siglo XXI?* (pp. 114–137). Mexico, D.F., Mexico: Siglo XXI.

Gordon, S., & Millán, R. (2004). Capital social: Una lectura de tres perspectivas clásicas. *Revista Mexicana de Sociología, 66*(4), 711–747. <http://www.revistas.unam.mx/index.php/rms/article/view/6002> Accessed 16.08.09.

Goudard, M., & Lubrano, M. (2010). Human capital, social capital and scientific production. <http://www3.eeg.uminho.pt/economia/nipe/workshopresearch/papers/Lubrano.pdf> Accessed 16.08.09.

Goudard, M., & Lubrano, M. (2013). Human capital, social capital and scientific research in Europe: An application of linear hierarchical models. *The Manchester School, 81*(6), 876–903. Available from http://dx.doi.org/10.1111/j.1467-9957.2012.02331.x.

Grubler, A., & Nemet, G. (2013). *Energy technology innovation: Learning from historical successes and failures*. Cambridge, England: Cambridge University Press.

Ibarra, A. (2009). Redes epistémicas: nuevos sujetos de la ciencia en nuevos modos de acción cognitiva. In F. Broncano, & A. Pérez (Eds.), *La ciencia y sus sujetos: ¿Quiénes hacen la ciencia del siglo XXI?* (pp. 135–158). Mexico, D.F., Mexico: Siglo XXI.

Jonsson, L., Baraldi, E., Larsson, L. E., Forsberg, P., & Severinsson, F. (2015). Targeting academic engagement in open innovation: Tools, effects and challenges for university management. *Journal of the Knowledge Economy, 6*(3), 522–550. Available from http://dx.doi.org/10.1007/s13132-015-0254-7.

Kucharþíkováa, A., Tokarþíkováa, E., & Blaškováa, M. (2015). Human capital management: Aspect of the human capital efficiency in university education. *Procedia: Social and Behavioral Sciences, 177*, 48–60. Available from http://dx.doi.org/10.1016/j.sbspro.2015.02.332.

Larner, W. (2015). Globalizing Knowledge networks: Universities, diaspora strategies, and academic intermediaries. *Geoforum, 59*, 197–205. Available from http://dx.doi.org/10.1016/j.geoforum.2014.10.006.

Liebowitz, J., & Suen, C. (2000). Developing Knowledge management metrics for measuring intellectual capital. *Journal of Intellectual Capital, 1*(1), 54–67. Available from http://dx.doi.org/10.1108/14691930010324160.

López-Leyva, S. (2014). Las universidades en la economía del conocimiento. *Revista de la Educación Superior, 43*(170), 153–160. <http://www.scielo.org.mx/scielo.php?script=sci_arttext&pid=S0185-27602014000200008> Accessed 16.08.09.

Meza-Rodríguez, N. (2010). *Análisis de los indicadores de la economía del conocimiento en las instituciones de educación superior pública en México (Master Thesis)*. Mexico, D.F., Mexico: Instituto Politécnico Nacional.

Núñez-Guerrero, Y., & Rodríguez-Monroy, C. (2014). Árboles de clasificación para jerarquizar los recursos intangibles asociados a la innovación en las instituciones de educación superior latinoamericanas. *Interciencia, 39*(4), 149–155. <http://www.redalyc.org/articulo.oa?id=33930206003> Accessed 16.08.09.

Olsen, D. (2015). Are there learning agents in innovative firms? A study of the potential role of human resource managers in learning and innovation. *Journal of the Knowledge Economy*, 7(3), 644–658. Available from http://dx.doi.org/10.1007/s13132-015-0252-9.

Organisation for Economic Co-operation and Development (1996). *The knowledge-based economy*. Paris, France: OECD.

Ortega y Gasset, J. (2007). *Misión de la universidad*. Madrid, Spain: Biblioteca Nueva.

Paulin, D., & Suneson, K. (2012). Knowledge transfer, knowledge sharing and knowledge barriers: Three blurry terms in KM. *The Electronic Journal of Knowledge Management, 10*(1), 81–91. <http://publications.lib.chalmers.se/publication/156127-knowledge-transfer-knowledge-sharing-and-knowledge-barriers-three-blurry-terms-in-km> Accessed 16.08.09.

Psarras, J. (2006). Education and training in the knowledge-based economy. *VINE: The Journal of Information and Knowledge Management Systems, 36*(1), 85–96. Available from http://dx.doi.org/10.1108/03055720610667390.

Ramírez, Y., Tejeda, A., & Garduño, S. (2013). Recognition of intellectual capital importance in the university sector. *International Journal of Business and Social Research, 3*(4), 27–41. <http://thejournalofbusiness.org/index.php/site/article/view/27> Accessed 16.08.09.

Ramírez-Córcoles, Y., Santos-Peñalver, S., & Tejeda, A. (2011). Intellectual capital in Spanish public universities: Stakeholders' information needs. *Journal of Intellectual Capital, 12*(3), 356–376. Available from http://dx.doi.org/10.1108/14691931111154689.

Ritzer, G., & Jurgenson, N. (2010). Production, consumption, prosumption: The nature of capitalism in the age of the digital 'prosumer'. *Journal of Consumer Culture, 10*(1), 13–36. Available from http://dx.doi.org/10.1177/1469540509354673.

Roberts, J. (2009). The global knowledge economy in question. *Critical Perspectives on International Business, 5*(4), 285–303. Available from http://dx.doi.org/10.1108/17422040911003033.

Rodríguez-Castellanos, A., Araujo-de-la-Mata, A., & Urrutia-Gutiérrez, J. (2001). La gestión del conocimiento científico-técnico en la universidad: Un caso y un proyecto. *Cuadernos de Gestión, 1*(1), 13–30. <https://addi.ehu.es/handle/10810/6883> Accessed 16.08.09.

Roos, G., Bainbridge, A., & Jacobsen, K. (2001). Intellectual capital as a strategic tool. *Strategy & Leadership, 29*(4), 21–26. Available from http://dx.doi.org/10.1108/10878570110400116.

Sánchez, E. (2006). Intellectual capital in universities: Improving transparency and internal management. *Journal of Intellectual Capital,* 7(4), 529–1458. Available from http://dx.doi.org/10.1108/14691930610709158.

Sánchez-Medina, A., Melián-González, A., & Hormiga-Pérez, E. (2007). El concepto de capital intelectual y sus dimensiones. *Investigaciones Europeas de Dirección y Economía de la Empresa, 13*(2), 97–111. <http://www.redalyc.org/articulo.oa?id=274120280005> Accessed 16.08.09.

Secundo, G., Margherita, A., Elia, G., & Passiante, G. (2010). Intangible assets in higher education and research: Mission, performance or both? *Journal of Intellectual Capital, 2*(11), 140–157. Available from http://dx.doi.org/10.1108/14691931011039651.

Slaughter, S., & Leslie, L. (2001). Expanding and elaborating the concept of academic capitalism. *Organization Overviews, 8*(2), 154–161. Available from http://dx.doi.org/10.1177/1350508401082003.

Slaughter, S., & Rhoades, G. (2009). *Academic capitalism and the new economy: Markets, sate, and higher education.* New York, USA: Johns Hopkins University Press.

Svare, H. (2016). User-producer dialogue, workplace innovation, and knowledge in a regional innovation system. *Journal of the Knowledge Economy,* 7(2), 565–586. Available from http://dx.doi.org/10.1007/s13132-014-0229-0.

Terra, L. (2007). *Diseminación del conocimiento académico en América Latina.* <http://www.unesco.org.uy/shs/fileadmin/templates/shs/archivos/anuario2007/articulo_15.pdf> Accessed 16.08.09.

Todericiua, R., & Serbana, A. (2015). Intellectual capital and its relationship with universities. *Procedia Economics and Finance, 27*, 713–717. Available from http://dx.doi.org/10.1016/S2212-5671(15)01052-7.

Tsui, L., Chapman, C., Schnirer, L., & Stewart, S. (2006). *A handbook on knowledge sharing: Strategies and recommendations for researchers, policymakers, and service providers.* Alberta, Canada: Community-University Partnership.

Txapartegui, E. (2009). ¿Sujeto-red o sujeto-programa? Consideraciones críticas a la propuesta de A. Ibarra. In F. Broncano, & A. Pérez (Eds.), *La ciencia y sus sujetos: ¿Quiénes hacen la ciencia del siglo XXI?* (pp. 164–180). Mexico, D.F., Mexico: Siglo XXI.

United Nations Environment Programme (2016). *The adaptation knowledge initiative.* Nairobi, Kenya: UNEP.

Vega-Encabo, J. (2009). Sujetos, objetividad y razón pública. In F. Broncano, & A. Pérez (Eds.), La ciencia y sus sujetos: ¿Quiénes hacen la ciencia del siglo XXI? *Mexico, D.F.* Mexico: Siglo XXI.

Whitley, R. (2008). Constructing universities as strategic actors: Limitations and variations. In L. Engwall, & D. Weaire (Eds.), *The university in the market* (pp. 23–37). London, England: Portland Press.

World Bank (2003). *Lifelong learning in the global knowledge economy: Challenges for developing countries: A World Bank report.* Washington, DC, USA: World Bank. <http://siteresources.worldbank.org/INTLL/Resources/Lifelong-Learning-in-the-Global-Knowledge-Economy/lifelonglearning_GKE.pdf> Accessed 16.08.09.

World Bank (2007). *Development studies building knowledge economies advanced strategies for development.* Washington, DC, USA: World Bank.

Yu, D., & Zhou, R. (2015). Intellectual management: An integrative theory. *Journal of the Knowledge Economy,* 1–28. Available from http://dx.doi.org/10.1007/s13132-015-0305-0.

CHAPTER 2

Conceptualization of Scientific Productivity, Production, Dissemination, and Communication

2.1 INTRODUCTION

The science that is not communicated does not exist. This premise implies that scientific knowledge is produced first and then it is communicated, but also that a large amount of contents and findings can remain indefinitely in a production phase. Without underestimating their importance, these contents which were not communicated become sources of reference of much reduced groups, especially when they are used in classroom teaching processes. However, they are never made available to the general public through scientific dissemination publications, or to scientific communities through scientific communication processes.

A systematic strengthening of scientific production guarantees that other knowledge generation processes take place (scientific dissemination and communication). A crucial factor should not be ignored: the existence of scientific learning paths and of scientific information for various stakeholders. This implies a way of implementing and ensuring the generational renewal of knowledge creation. In the countries with more capital (economic, social, intellectual), there is a high correlation between their capital and their levels of scientific leadership. This is because they have sought to train citizens that are capable of using and producing science, thereby offering various opportunities and conditions for intellectual work to happen; this situation should be emulated by developing countries.

The actions that every country should follow for achieving the systematic generation of knowledge and for appreciating science as a key element for progress are: (1) maintain access to state-of-the-art scientific information resources; (2) link national scientific goals with the characteristics of the scientific research conducted in the country; (3) create

The Role of Information Professionals in the Knowledge Economy
DOI: http://dx.doi.org/10.1016/B978-0-12-811222-9.00002-9

mechanisms to foster a social interest in promoting science and its use; (4) multiply professional and scientific resources; and (5) increase the scientific literacy of all citizens (Gutiérrez-Vargas, 2002). It can be considered that scientific information, learning, and professional training are three key elements for the growth of scientific literature; as well as influencing the potential for countries to achieve it.

Therefore, scientific and technology creation become crucial elements for the development of institutions and countries. However, economic conditions will determine the challenges each country has to face, especially those related to the infrastructure consolidation in higher education and research institutions (knowledge institutions). Knowledge generation will stimulate an increase in the educational level, which will bring forth new social demands, such as higher-paid jobs that would recognize new professional skills or consumption processes of new goods and services as byproducts of the development taking place (Pérez-Cazares, 2013).

The starting point for knowledge generation is scientific production, which involves a number of actors and efforts for it to occur formally through institutional, statewide, and national scientific policies. Such efforts are assessed by analyzing the dimensions demanded by scientific production in three levels or coordinated axes of participation: (1) science policy and the definition of a research and development system; (2) audit of each knowledge institution regarding their guidelines for research work; (3) integration and formation of research groups in a proper structure (Albornoz, 2007; Izquierdo-Alonso, Moreno-Fernández, & Izquierdo-Arroyo, 2008; Martín-Serrano, 2006; Nieto, 1995; Scheunemann de Souza, 2006). These three aspects will result in the generation of scientific production and communication models, the restructuring of institutional management processes and the individual measurement of each researcher's competence.

Once these three fundamental elements are achieved within each knowledge institution, it should start displaying a more complex perspective towards its exterior. This perspective should include the following considerations, which cannot be controlled but demand adaptability: the globalization experienced by society in general; the emergence of the knowledge society and its requirements; and rapid change, aspects known as the new paradigm of knowledge production (Moravec, 2007). This makes it appropriate to include the review of educational theories, basically constructivism, as new knowledge is integrated through different interpretations of reality. Paradoxically, the population that is able to understand and apply knowledge to solve problems is drastically reduced, as capable population is inversely proportional to the excess of knowledge generated (Semir, 2010).

Scientific dissemination and communication through scientific knowledge and as results of research processes, can become a potential or effective power for large groups, according to the special interests that may exist. Such influence of the scientific knowledge should not be elitist, reserved only to scientific communities and political groups in power (Erazo-Pesántez, 2009), but to society in general. Throughout this chapter, the various concepts related to scientific knowledge generation processes are pointed out and differentiated: scientific productivity, scientific production, academic production, scientific communication, and scientific dissemination. Despite the fact that each concept is fundamental for the institutions related to knowledge generation, the one that is more developed due to its interest within this book is scientific communication, because it contains the products that are recognized by the experts of scientific communities, as they define the continued growth of knowledge.

Knowledge generation has multiple implications in its efforts to identify and classify its dimensions and concepts. The measurement of scientific productivity capabilities should be analyzed from an individual perspective over the skills each participating individual has, and globally, over the capabilities of organizations, countries, and disciplines. This allows to develop actions for promoting and encouraging research and the generation of new scientific and technological developments, the capacity for managing scientific products, and finding ways for collectively sharing knowledge.

2.2 THE VALUE OF SCIENTIFIC CREATION AND THE ROLE OF KNOWLEDGE INSTITUTIONS

Since the 1980s and 1990s, a process of redefining the role of the professor as a researcher within the knowledge institutions began, and the main formal element enabling such function was identified: the value of the knowledge generator through research. Professors are considered productive as long as they can balance teaching, institutional management services, community services, and research (Bailey, 1992).

The value of research should be included in institutional priorities schemes, but scientific communication is not yet universally considered part of it, neither in its entire dimension. In an ideal case, identifying the value of scientific communication starts by understanding two fundamental principles: (1) considering that is not necessarily an activity of independent workers (though these cases exist), but of individuals that are formally affiliated with a knowledge institution; and (2) the need to define, characterize, and quantify the productivity of each member from a teaching and research body, identifying their productivity levels according to their specific activities (Thurston, 1981).

Measuring the productivity of teachers and researchers in knowledge institutions has multiple implications and a variety of options. A concrete model for measuring productivity considers the following aspects: (1) scientific production must become a core and daily process in higher education; (2) performance must be quantified using a formal metric, which has to determine its own conception of productivity; (3) the measurement of quality should be central for assessing productivity and it should be prioritized over quantity, but without ignoring the latter (Sullivan, Mackie, Massy, & Sinha, 2012).

Any measurement model will have multiple limitations, as they are composed of diverse elements beyond the scientific products generated. The perspectives of the scientific production and communication environments include the following specific measurement characteristics: (1) fostering joint production, considering the number of products and especially the interaction among teachers and researchers that makes such production possible; (2) the nurturing of higher training levels for researchers will cause high variability in the quality and characteristics of the scientific communication; (3) the quality of productivity depends on the relationships between materials or inputs and results or outputs of the products generated; (4) the products generated managed to pass from the condition of scientific production to that of scientific communication, since it is complex to measure the products that remained on the level of creation, without arriving at their formal scientific communication (Sullivan et al., 2012).

Scientific production and communication processes acquire sufficient value after the institution that generated them is recognized for its prestige from its knowledge infrastructure and for achieving a position in university quality rankings. This allows to compare institutions, states, or countries, although there may be inaccuracies caused by variations that depend on the characteristics of the scientific disciplines that each entity studies or prioritizes. In order to ensure that knowledge generation purposes are achieved, the following elements must be present: motivators for researchers; sense of organizational ownership and identity; ability to participate in "invisible colleges" and scientific subcultures; scientific rewards schemes offered by the institutions; technology for scientific work; organizational legitimacy of the knowledge generation function (Bailey, 1992; Canales & Luna, 2003; Díaz-Barriga & Rigo, 2003; García-Cepero, 2007; Feldmann, 2005; Hernández-Castañón, García-Valenzuela, Uicab-Pool, Calini, & Mendes, 2008; Kinsella, 1997; Leslie, 2002; Marsh & Hattie, 2002).

Fundamentally, knowledge institutions are associated with the training of human resources at a professional level and, as a result, to the development of knowledge transfer processes (Fernández-Aquino & Valdés-Puentes, 2008; Torres-Rodríguez, 2013). The new conceptions of universities have overcome the above, since society currently demands their actions to be based upon four key processes: university administration and management, teaching, extension, and scientific research (Chauí, 2001; Kennedy, 1997). Current educational policies may prioritize scientific research through the generation of publications, thus becoming one of the core activities of knowledge institutions.

Knowledge institutions' positioning depends, to a large extent and in a somewhat ideal scenario, on ensuring that knowledge production and generation is a process with the following characteristics: it has dynamic results; it has a personal, group, organizational, and social sense; it is based upon perception, understanding, creative reprocessing; and knowledge applications and possible transformation are conceived with the purpose of communicating information, which is represented in various sources and media (Núñez-Paula, 2004). Knowledge generation is determined by three fundamental aspects: (1) it should be a seamless process, developed on a daily basis; (2) it is a result of the continuous and dynamic influences that people receive, it is based on accumulated experiences and the possibility of transferring it to researchers in training (students) is considered; (3) the existence of patterns of cultural formation and social values in the organizations is inexorable, but some institutions will prioritize research development over these other aspects (Albornoz, 2007).

The distribution of the knowledge generated will depend on economic, demographic, cultural, and technological factors. The conditions may vary between countries but also between institutions in different countries or even between institutions within the same country.

Therefore, the differences regarding rates of consumption and of scientific production turn knowledge generation into an activity with an economic connotation (Middaugh, 2001; Saavedra-Fernández, 2002). Then, the conditions that foster knowledge generation among professors go beyond their own interests, including those elements that govern their work, social, and infrastructure environments.

As social institutions, knowledge institutions enable the retention and accumulation of knowledge developed by their social gatherings, but the efforts to share and distribute knowledge will depend on the professors themselves (Berger & Luckmann, 2001). The publication of scientific findings goes beyond ordinary facts or mere personal interests. It implies having the adequate training to do so, using the appropriate channels for it, the proximity or distance in which knowledge is disseminated (whether they are publications of national or international reach), the use of semantic elements that are part of the rigor demanded by the scientific societies that can accept or reject academic products that aim to be published. Then, to sustain knowledge generation as an everyday activity of professors and researchers, the capacity possessed by individuals and the institutions in which they operate must be evaluated. As part of their capacities to sustain knowledge generation, institutions tend to ensure the availability of a certain amount of information resources to researchers. These resources facilitate better theoretical foundations for scientific production, in addition to offering clear benefits for generating research (Altamirano-Sánchez, 2006; Middaugh, 2001).

Currently, the growth of universities is being measured not so much in terms of their mass enrollment or the mere acknowledgment of teaching as their main activity. Instead, measurement must contemplate the initiatives undertaken for the development of teachers capable of generating scientific production through dissemination and communication activities. Such production is expected to have a positive and direct influence on increasing education quality in general, and in particular of the teaching that takes place within universities (Brown & McCartney, 1998; Sharobeam & Howard, 2002; Vogt, 2004). The conventional argument about how research supports teaching within higher education institutions is that, when research is encouraged and students are involved in it, they should use research findings to improve their understanding of the topics covered in class in ways that are clearer and closer to them. Unfortunately, this does not happen so often because of curricula's rigidity, which limits the possibilities of including new materials.

The combination of research and teaching can be a way to change the traditional teaching and learning paradigm that consists of models based on information transmission from professors to students (Badley, 2002). The link between research and teaching depends on the nature of professors and on their classroom learning experiences, which offer them the possibility of establishing such a connection (Brew, 2003; Elton, 2001). Professors should integrate their research to the contexts of their classes in order to improve them, by emulating procedures from their own research within their academic activities; therefore, scientific research should not be dissociated from teaching processes (Prince, Felder, & Brent, 2007; Seymour, Hunter, Laursen, & Deantoni, 2004).

2.3 MAIN CONCEPTUALIZATIONS RELATED TO THE KNOWLEDGE GENERATION PROCESSES

Throughout this chapter, the words science and knowledge are used almost interchangeably. However, the latter has diverse dimensions and is deemed to belong within science—or be scientific—when it has been accepted, systematized, and validated by the scientific community. Knowledge is scientific if it is generated by scientifically literate individuals that followed scientific processes to build it (Raviolo, Ramírez, López, & Aguilar, 2010).

Science is a knowledge-generating activity. Both research and communication are considered essential parts of the scientific production process and, therefore, their methods are intertwined and connected (Maletta, 2009). The result is knowledge generation, which must have certain characteristics: subjectivity–objectivity, it has transfer capacity, it is reinforced at every step of its development, it is spontaneous and perishable according to the obsolescence ranges of each discipline (Treat, 2008).

There are precise procedures that must be followed for knowledge generation to occur, they must be accurately understood, although they are not necessarily used in such a specific way within the literature reviewed. These basic procedures for knowledge generation are: (1) scientific productivity, (2) scientific production, (3) academic production, (4) scientific communication, and (5) scientific dissemination. According to a review of the published literature, these terms are often used indiscriminately, even as synonyms, so it is necessary to differentiate by providing their definitions and scopes. Fig. 2.1 dimensions the concepts mentioned above and illustrates how they relate to the institutional environment, society in general, and scientific communities.

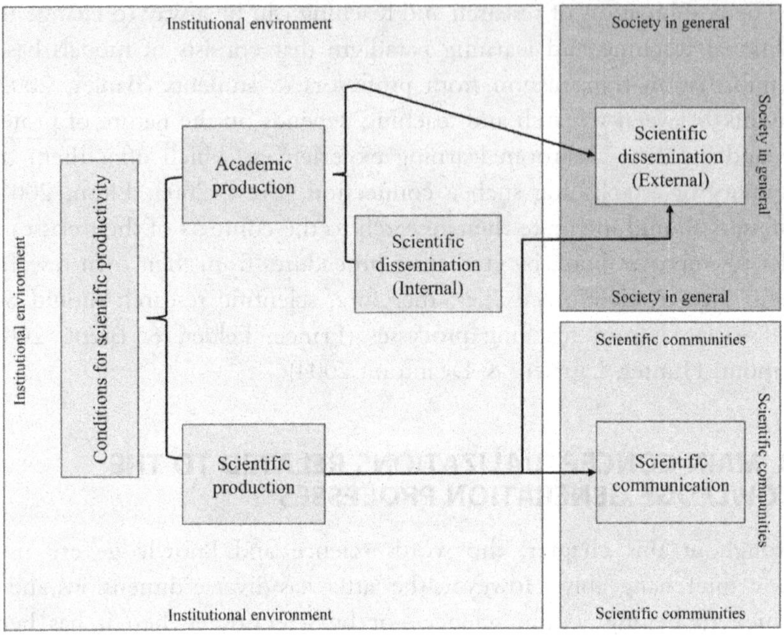

Figure 2.1 Model of the knowledge generation process.

2.3.1 Scientific Productivity

Scientific productivity is the measurement of the knowledge institutions' behavior regarding the fostered environment for scientific culture and activities to take place. This concept usually has a strong psychological connotation, which turns the knowledge generation processes in compulsory and systematic actions according to the fostered organizational environment, where institutional perception has the vision of increasing its intellectual development (Sonpal-Valias, 1996). The definition of scientific productivity depends on the identification of different environments and indicators for knowledge generation:

1. *Record.* A basic aspect that must be met in order to use scientific productivity measurement models is to record the development of patents and publications made by researchers from the knowledge institution, including their quality and prestige levels (i.e., indexed journals have more prestige) as well as the number of citations made to each publication (Doellefeld, 1998; Gonzalez-Argote, Garcia-Rivero, & Dorta-Contreras, 2016; Matzinger-Tchakerian, 1996; Treat, 2008).

2. *Index of relative productivity.* Scientific productivity measurement models should be based on productivity rates, which are the sum of the published products divided by the number of researchers per institution or country, resulting in a number that allows to conduct fairer comparisons between institutions and their scientific behavior patterns (Matzineger-Tchakerian, 1996). This aspect is known as "relative productivity," which makes it possible to develop comparative analyses within similar environments, which are not necessarily the ideal ones (Tarango, Hernández-Gutiérrez, & Vázquez-Guzmán, 2015).
3. *Conditions defined by the knowledge institution.* Measuring scientific productivity depends on three factors that each institution can define if they apply to it: (1) general results that enable the institution to be compared regarding competitiveness with other entities are promoted; (2) academic institutions value that their professors decide to devote themselves only to teaching or to research; and (3) productivity is measured according to the number of published products (Sonpal-Valias, 1996).
4. *Holistic evaluation of scientific productivity.* The scenarios that enable the generation of a scientific culture must consider the productivity of teachers holistically: teaching activities are compulsory, there is a necessary balance between research and teaching, professors participate in institutional management activities and they publish research products (Alli, 2002; Jennings, 1997; Weiss, 1998). The institutional vision must start from the individual measurement of each researcher, which must consider different kinds of evidences that can be easily quantified and evaluated qualitatively: (1) every product that is considered scientific communication, including peer-reviewed articles, conference proceedings, books, book chapters, patents, and other published research documents; (2) evidences of the professors' work impact, such as a list of citations to their publications and invitations to participate in events, academic activities of collegial bodies, research groups, or editorial boards, as well as the peer reviews they have conducted for scientific journals or professional conferences; (3) other academic merits related to obtaining grants or funding for research and awards as researchers; (4) advancements that demonstrate their continuing research activity, including evidences of products accepted for publication or in-press. Collective work in processes of scientific productivity will influence the direction of organizational change (Howell, 2000).

5. *Students' participation in scientific activities.* Researchers are considered the main actors in scientific activities. However, it is also necessary to measure the participation of students, especially graduate students, in the processes of research and publication (Gonzalez-Argote et al., 2016). The composition of a scientific profile is based on various aspects and depends on the characteristics of the published sources: full name, institutional affiliation, country affiliation, email, areas of research, and recognition of what has already been published (Alcántara, 2009; Martin, 2009; Trillo-Tinoco, 2015).
6. *Subjective measurements.* Subjective aspects for measuring scientific productivity environments include personal characteristics of researchers, institutional environment factors, members' interactions effects, quality of scientific products, the educational perspectives of both the person and the institution, and the productivity regarding academic and research activities. The academic quality ranking of the institution is also often considered (Alli, 2002); as well as academic culture and subcultures, capacities for adapting to change, and the characteristics of collegial interactions (Weiss, 1998).
7. *The institutionalization of science.* Scientific productivity ranks as an autonomous activity that is carried out for scientific growth. Institutionalizing the role of a science professional and of the social and individual conditions will influence an organizational change toward scientific growth. The institutionalization of science is like a professional career that will allow institutional and personal growth, as long as specific working norms are defined (Osegueda, 2003).
8. *Institutional development of scientific productivity.* The manner and style in which scientific productivity happens in knowledge institutions will vary depending on the type of institution. If it is a research institution, research is a priority over teaching, while two scenarios can happen in universities: (1) they have scientific centers (focused on research); and (2) professors develop teaching and research simultaneously. Therefore, structural circumstances are more or less favorable depending on the condition of each institution (Boardman, 2006).
9. *Institutional or regional environment.* Measuring scientific productivity has a high relationship with the institutional or regional environment, hence, it is possible to identify the value and the economic, social, and cultural push in every government effort regarding public policies (Bustos, 2010); which requires scientific products that are designed and characterized by the environment (Mugnaini, 2006).

As interrelated concepts regarding scientific knowledge generation, scientific production and scientific communication include the academic, infrastructure, and scientific culture environments, allowing the global measurement of scientific productivity in institutions. A particular scientific productivity measurement model can be implemented from the institutional scientific behavior and by identifying the following six general dimensions, which have their own evaluation criteria: (1) knowledge generation processes: the record of indexed, peer-reviewed and scientific dissemination articles; (2) professors' academic quality: academic degrees and quality certifications as researchers and professors; (3) the impact of scientific communication: first author, number of citations and of institutional and regional collaborations; (4) capacity for innovation through patents applied for and registered, as well as any other record of innovation capabilities; (5) areas of professional practice: collective work, type of contract for researchers, quality of the accredited academic programs where researchers collaborate; and (6) institutional capacity for the management of scientific publications: generating their own high-quality scientific publications (Tarango et al., 2015; Universidad Nacional Autónoma de México, Dirección General de Evaluación Institucional [UNAM], 2016).

2.3.2 Scientific Production

This concept mainly refers to the publication or dissemination of the scientific advances conducted by a professor or researcher. Scientific production has the status of published (for documents) or presented (presentations, conferences, or keynotes), but other definitions are also common, such as *in press*, *under peer-review*, or *under review*. The latter denominations would mean that the scientific production under any of the mentioned status has not yet been made available for scientific communities or society in general, although they are in a procedure or state that will make them available soon.

Scientific production functions as an industrial metaphor to represent knowledge as a social process, therefore, scientists take certain prime materials and transform them into products (Maletta, 2009). In this sense, there is the pretension that research processes' results must be the greatest number of products that an individual can produce in a given period (Porter & Umbach, 2001).

Not all products generated through scientific production will become scientific communication. Those that become scientific communication are called formal scientific production, while the rest are informal scientific production. Regularly, traditional indicators and metrics for measuring scientific production only record formal scientific production, excluding some of the activities that are conducted by professors in the universities and hence, scientific production is not recorded faithfully to its full extent (Braga, Bernardete, & Silva, 2003). Some actions included in professors' scientific production, but not necessarily considered important, include: the number of supervised student research projects during a certain period of time; research-related incentives or awards received by their students; the lecturing and grading workload the professor has, and even the number of theses supervisions. The latter action involves the thesis as a product that has the condition of a manuscript or document not published, which is often developed over the course of several years before the final product is ready and therefore it does not usually manage to be scientific communication (especially if it is not made available online), unless scientific articles, books, book chapters, and presentations are derived from the thesis.

Both in terms of scientific production and scientific communication, not every element evaluated has the same weight. Especially in scientific production, there are items that are not assessed nor are they among the core processes of science, but they are directly related to the access to resources and recognition, they are excessively bureaucratized administrative actions such as scientific dissemination, development of institutional publications, and creating educational materials (Albornoz, 2007).

Scientific production and scientific communication are actually two complementary phases divided by a fine line, but without the former the second cannot occur. Both represent the product of scientific activity and lead to new knowledge, thereby creating scientific capital; which is of crucial importance in knowledge institutions (Shults, 2005). Results obtained from productive activities are presented and communicated, but in different moments either formal or informal channels can be chosen in the social-historical practice (Campos-Rosas, 2000).

Scientific production includes all kinds of academic and scientific activities; it is the materialization of the knowledge generated regularly through experimentation and the consultation of other documents (Piedra-Salomón & Martínez-Rodríguez, 2007). Therefore, science is not spontaneously conceived, but its roots are linked to knowledge institutions and their quality, and broadly related to innovation, creativity, and inquiry (Salas-Perea, 2000).

However, there are exceptions of science conducted by researchers not affiliated with any knowledge institution (independent researchers) or by researchers located at the periphery of the institutions they are affiliated with but that does not recognize the value of research nor does it appropriately foster the conditions for generating a scientific culture ("outsiders"). The research quality in the latter case might be good and, if it is, it will not reflect the values and quality of the knowledge institution regarding research, but it would far exceed them. This kind of scientific production could be seen as an anomaly, but it would also represent the case of an intellectual capital that a knowledge institution might lose easily.

Arguably, scientific production has less quantifiable value when informal media are used for its communication, which is different in the case of the formally published and transmitted products conducted through scientific communication, which involves formal media. It is important to take this into consideration, because professors and researchers might resort to various areas to disseminate their research findings, albeit with low visibility, in three basic forms: (1) within their workplace and their own academic community, with other professors, scientists, as well as with students and research groups; (2) informal knowledge transfer to other organizations that may influence their investigations; and (3) those informal media used to highlight their research findings to society in general (Altamirano-Sánchez, 2006).

The conceptualization approaches of scientific production are too varied and they generally just identify those products that are publishable. The literature suggests the following classification: (1) scientific production, which includes documents for supporting teaching, university-printed documents, reviews, reports, translations, videos, prototypes and other physical products, artistic works, awards, reports or technical reports presented to various national, international, governmental, and private institutions, in addition to undergraduate and graduate theses; (2) scientific communication, comprising scientific articles published in national and international journals, books presenting research results, textbooks, compilations of chapters written by experts, extensive monographs on different scientific subjects, and patents; and (3) scientific dissemination, consisting of writings of expository nature, conferences presented at scientific congresses and conferences, participations in science fairs, publications in newspapers, and other informal communication media (Maletta, 2009; Olivas-Ávila & Musi-Lechuga, 2013; Ospina-Rúa & Toro-Botero, 2009).

The development of scientific production demands concrete actions related to inventions, innovations, and dissemination (Jiménez, Rangel, & Albornoz, 2004). In recent times, the incorporation of digital media has generated various means of informal communication (Banús, 2006), such as social media, blogs, and wikis. Using these media, researchers share their activities with colleagues from all latitudes, giving rise to thematic networks or information products made collectively between individuals, institutions, and nations, for disseminating scientific production among the members of different collaboration clusters (Liu, 2010; Prat, 1998, 2006). Scientific production and its ICT-based informal transfer media happen according to three perspectives: (1) technological networks; (2) social media with some user segmentation; and (3) knowledge networks, which are selective in including only specialized users (Morales-Campos & Martínez-Arellano, 2011; Polanco, 2006; Schiavo, 2006). According to Maletta (2009), the conceptualization of scientific production has the following precise characteristics, which summarize the above described, but also serve to clarify and expand the concept with other elements:

1. It is a social process that occurs in an organized and institutionalized manner, its main protagonists are the scientific communities (physical and virtual), through which ideas, data, problems, hypotheses, theories, questions, and answers are generated, discussed, and criticized.
2. It covers diverse activities ranging from the development and discussion of concepts and theoretical stances, the collection and analysis of empirical data before they are turned to formal documents used for scientific communication. This means that the products have not yet been validated by the scientific community. After undergoing a strict peer-review procedure, the documents are published and only then can they be considered part of scientific communication.
3. It involves theoretical reflection, the research and analysis of data using scientific research methods, either at a theoretical or empirical level.

2.3.3 Academic Production

According to the literature, it is the least used expression among the set of concepts discussed in this chapter, and it is frequently used as a synonym for scientific production (Townsend & Rosser, 2007). However, academic production is part of scientific production, it emerges with the intention of being used in academic media, but their contributions are so significant that it ends up being edited for the purpose of being published in scientific dissemination media, both formal and informal.

The correct use of the term academic production generates some conceptual controversies among the perspectives of different authors, which in turn allow to define it and limit its scope. The main contributions toward its definition are summarized as follows:

1. It represents a small part of the scientific production, it does not include all teaching activities, and not every activity that is included within academic production may be applicable in most scientific disciplines (Bland, Center, Finstad, & Risbey, 2005).
2. It is understood as a set of activities that professors integrate while developing their classes, for example, the number of students trained or number of research projects supervised during a given period (Crosta & Packman, 2005).
3. It is formed by the activities that professors and researchers develop with the purpose of enriching teaching processes and their impact is confined to their own institution (López-Carrasco, 2013).
4. According to Maletta (2009), academic production and scientific production are synonymous and are used interchangeably. Although, some products are often seen as typical of academic production, this is when its contents do not demonstrate their scientific value with empirical data; something that occurs mainly in the humanities and social sciences. Meanwhile, in the case of the natural sciences, when academic activities have practical applications, these are considered scientific production. Under this concept, the "academic" could be disregarded next to the "scientific" perception of some products.

A complementary view over the conceptualization of academic production can be summarized in its following components: (1) the set of works (published and unpublished) of professors and researchers, undergraduate and graduate students, and from those developing research activities in their field; (2) theses, dissertations, and documents that validate the end of an academic program, both at undergraduate and graduate levels; (3) works published by the editorial departments of the institutions where academic bodies and research centers are grouped; (4) course syllabi, courses, and seminars, as well as the curricula of higher education programs; and (5) approved documents of research and extension projects, working projects, results and progress reports, and information generated in research centers (Fushimi, Mallo, & Pichinini, 2005).

2.3.4 Scientific Communication

This concept represents the availability of publications through digital or print media, previously approved through peer review, which has the role of serving as a quality filter. Scientific communication purposes are to provide the availability for consulting these products, in addition to nurturing the knowledge within a scientific discipline, according to the demands of its scientific community.

The documents made available through scientific communication come from knowledge creation through research processes, which include activities of scientific production. The scientific communication phase is essential in the knowledge generation process, because it allows validating scientific results by subjecting them to discussion and professional evaluation (Maletta, 2009). The involvement of scientific communities in the processes of scientific communication is essential, as they may analyze, reproduce, validate, and eventually accept, reject, or enrich the results from each researcher (Maletta, 2009).

Scientific communication consists of primary scientific discourses, which are produced by scientists for scientists. These primary scientific discourses which are published in scientific publications must not be confused with those scientific discourses that were developed for teaching (as these would correspond to academic production), nor with the scientific dissemination discourses that are aimed at general audiences (Malcher & Lopes, 2013).

Scientific communication is the process of presenting, distributing, and receiving scientific information within and for scientific societies, and it can be considered the basic mechanism for science's existence and development (Gutiérrez-Couto, Blanco-Pérez, & Casal-Acción, 2004). Scientific communication represents free communication among scientists. However, although it may happen in different forms and roads, only what makes use of formal channels is strictly considered scientific communication, mainly scientific journals (Mata-Acosta, 2008; National Academy of Science, 1982).

Scientific journals can be printed, digital, or hybrid, their format is not relevant, just their impact and quality (Morales-Campos & Martínez-Arellano, 2011). Although there are other media, the journal is considered the ideal formal mechanism for scientific communication. Its structure is a thematic or disciplinary compilation of contributions known as scientific articles, which are among the more preferred products regarding scientific communication. If the scientific journal issue is a thematic compilation, it contains articles dealing exclusively with a particular topic from various perspectives. Conversely, if it is a disciplinary compilation, it means that a central theme was not defined, so it contains articles on various topics that belong to a discipline or to related disciplines that are relevant to the scope and thematic coverage of the journal. The journal has the specific purpose of making research results, ideas, and debates public in a clear, concise, and accurate manner, so they are regarded as being at the frontiers of knowledge (Abadal-Falgueras & Ruis-Alcaraz, 2006; Luna-Morales & Russell-Barnard, 2009; Mata-Acosta, 2008).

Scientific communication can be generally understood as the number of publications or creations individually generated by a researcher. In this concept, it is especially important to consider the impact of such publications, which is traditionally measured by the number of citations obtained by the publications and is an indicator of the academic attention a scientific document has received within its discipline, institution, or any geographical area (Piedra-Salomón & Martínez-Rodríguez, 2007; Porter & Umbach, 2001). The main characteristics that distinguish scientific communication are summarized as follows:

1. It is a formal process by which scientists interact and create new knowledge. Publications are the formal medium for scientific communication, as other means may be considered invalid and hence not being seen as scientific communication (Hernández-Gutiérrez, 2014; Romanos de Tiratel, Contardi, & Giunti, 2010). The use of informal or semiformal media is often called scientific dissemination.
2. The measurement of impact as well as personal and institutional competitiveness in scientific communication cannot be limited only to counting the amount of published products, but its assessment will vary depending on each scientific discipline (Kling & McKim, 2000). However, it is obvious that measuring scientific productivity through the number of published articles encourages scientific publication and, therefore, the development of science (Campos-Rosas, 2000).
3. Scientific communication is a consequence of the completion of research processes. It is measured quantitatively and qualitatively through the bibliographic data of publications, the identification of the amount of citations obtained, the characteristics of individuals that participated in its creation, and the level of contribution that a certain product implies for the development of a scientific discipline (Braga et al., 2003; Piña-Pozas, 2007).
4. Publication is the formal scientific communication medium, but other means of communication that allow making it accessible to many members of scientific communities should also be considered, for example, full-text scientific databases, scientific information and

research services, public websites, digital libraries, repositories, meta search engines, and discovery services (Søndergaard, Andersen, & Hjørland, 2003).

2.3.5 Scientific Dissemination

The current growth experienced by the scientific production processes, in addition to the social commitment that distinguishes knowledge institutions, give rise to the challenge of improving the social distribution of knowledge processes, avoiding that knowledge becomes a privilege of the few, which generates some features of exclusivity for science, such as knowledge retention and accumulation without proper distribution (Altamirano-Sánchez, 2006).

Regarding knowledge, talking about *communication* and *dissemination* depends on the conditions in which content was expressed (level of complexity in discourse and language), the medium used in such expression (formal, semiformal, informal), and the definition of the audience it was directed to (specialized or the general public), in both cases, the constant is the magic word "science" (Vogt, 2004). Scientific dissemination is characterized by low density in terms of the discourse and language in which contents are expressed, by the use of semiformal or informal means, and for having the purpose of reaching a wider and not necessarily scientific audience. According Zamboni (2001), scientific dissemination is: (1) an activity of knowledge diffusion; (2) social sharing of knowledge without restrictive limits; and (3) represents the discursive restatement of certain scientific contents. For scientific knowledge producers, to define the spaces for scientific dissemination and scientific communication will largely depend on the intended visibility and the social value given to the scientific content (Daza & Aroleda, 2007). It should be noted that scientific dissemination and scientific communication are not mutually exclusive activities. Typically, much of the knowledge that is communicated though formal media is later disseminated through semiformal or informal means to ensure that society or at least a wider audience receives a return of the economic and moral investment that society has made in their academics, researchers, and knowledge institutions, which in turn should transfer their scientific findings to society. The media used for dissemination are lectures, scientific fairs or events, publishing in scientific dissemination magazines, news websites, blogs, wikis, or YouTube videos. However, it is not necessarily the authors of the research nor their institutions that assume the task of scientific dissemination, partly because scientific dissemination does not have the same value as scientific communication for the knowledge institutions or for scientific evaluation systems.

Both scientific communication and scientific dissemination usually have a certain bias in its measurement, assessment, and evaluation. In the case of the latter, bias manifests from the preference or priority given to the contents of certain disciplines such as natural sciences or engineering over the humanities and social sciences. This is because natural sciences and engineering have been legitimizing their methods and they represent a particular interest for the industrialization toward economic and social development (Mariscal-Orozco, 2007). However, it also denotes the lack or deficiencies of clear cultural policies in countries for promoting and encouraging knowledge transfer from all disciplines to the public. In fact, many models for the evaluation of scientific productivity do not contemplate scientific dissemination for any discipline or consider it of low value, so there is the perception that dissemination does not add value to individual or institutional scientific competitiveness.

It is important to reiterate that the manifestations of scientific dissemination are often varied, and although it is always mentioned that they are aimed at a lay audience, this should not be necessarily taken so literally or to its extreme. For example, expository writings, participations in scientific fairs, and presentations at conferences, are activities actually aimed at contributing within limited academic environments, from a potentially scientific population. The above activities are different from other dissemination media, such as scientific dissemination magazines, news websites, blogs, wikis, or YouTube videos, which are intended for individuals with little or no scientific training.

Measuring the quality of scientific dissemination from the modern positivist practice requires tangible products, and the spaces where they are best found is in mass media publications, especially print newspapers or digital media, which are related to scientific journalism. The quality of scientific dissemination information is difficult to measure. Although there are accurate metrics that are based on international standards to measure scientific communication, in the case of scientific dissemination, measurement is limited and focuses solely on the impact made to citizens or the views expressed by readers (Bustos-Mora, 2004; Teixeira-Batista, 2006). However, new broader attention indicators such as Altmetrics offer a feasible mechanism that can be applied to scientific dissemination.

Scientific journalism, which is synonymous with scientific dissemination only through the press, is a way of dissemination scientific and technological information for the general public in an accessible and decoded language (Alarcó-Hernández, 1999; Calvo-Hernando, 2001). Scientific journalism pretends to promote citizen participation, encouraging citizens to acquire scientific knowledge or at least a sensitivity towards science, knowledge, and its actors, in order to generate a positive impact on the current configuration and the future of societies through research findings, without requiring membership of an intellectual elite or scientific community, but contributing to the generation of a public scientific awareness (Avogadro, 2002; Moreno-Castro, 2003).

Most people, including scientists and science communicators, consider that scientific dissemination is the best way to process the information generated by researchers, for themselves and for journalists and media, with the purpose of sharing it with the general public (Bosch, 2011). Scientific dissemination has the same elements of a communication process (sender–message–receiver), with the difference that it involves the scientist or the communication professional, a content in simple or colloquial language, and the general public that does not necessarily require scientific training.

Conducting scientific dissemination demands precise skills, since the prime material is scientific knowledge, which must be transmitted to a nonspecialized audience, the resulting format demands a pleasant reformulation of science that should invite its appreciation, with the purpose of reducing scientific illiteracy and helping to develop and educate citizens (Beyer-Ruiz & Hernández-García, 2009; Herrera-Lima, 2007; Nakkazi, 2015; Sjøberg, 2002). The largest challenge for scientific dissemination is to change society's image of science, eliminating stale prejudices against its value and contributions (Belenguer-Jané, 2002) and stopping conceiving it as being far from social reality.

Fig. 2.2 summarizes the different stages of scientific dissemination and scientific communication, using a model based on the content developed for conceptualizing the new knowledge generation moments.

2.4 THE PRODUCTS OF SCIENTIFIC COMMUNICATION

Scientific communication has great importance for knowledge institutions because it represents the end of a knowledge generation process and it is the element that most feasibly allows the measurement of individual and

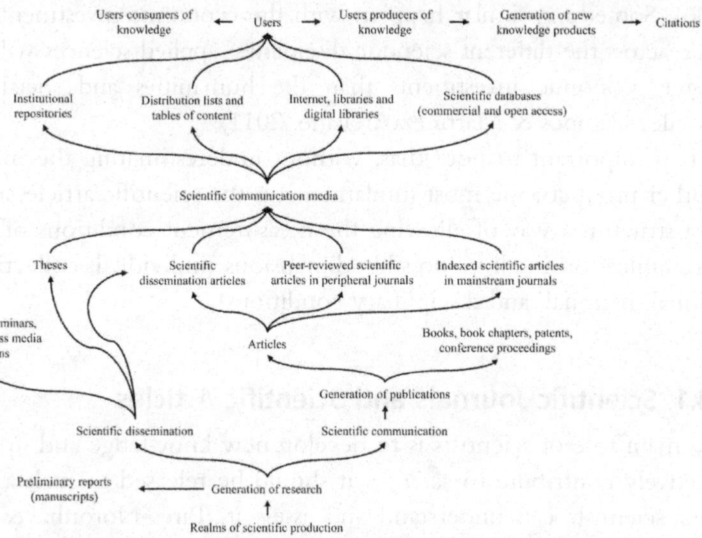

Figure 2.2 Scientific dissemination and scientific communication process.

collective competitiveness (research groups, institutions, countries, or disciplines). This section provides a description of the main products of scientific communication, their main features and their quality, structure, and influence conditions.

The products generated as scientific communication and that are used for its measurement are composed of various information sources demanded by publishing systems and scientific publishers, which establish different standards to evaluate them by taking into account the amount, consistency, and quality. Currently, the formats of the scientific products have changed dramatically, especially with the incorporation of information and communication technologies (ICT) in various educational contexts and of information science.

Despite the fact that apparently the quantity of product types that conform to scientific communication are reduced, it should be noted that they are the result of prior and hard work, involving research processes and facilitated by the existence of a complementary productivity environment that nurtures the academic and scientific work of professors or researchers. The preferred types of products tend to be chosen depending on the scientific discipline, for example, the resource most used in the humanities is the book, but professionals in the natural sciences and technological fields will systematically resort to scientific articles (Abadal-Falgueras & Ruis-Alcaraz,

2006). Something similar happens with the economic investments that are made across the different scientific disciplines: applied sciences will demand greater economic investments than the humanities and social sciences (Morales-Campos & Martínez-Arellano, 2011).

It is important to note that, without underestimating the importance of other products, the most fundamental is the scientific article, as it is the most structured way of allowing the measurement conditions of scientific communication in all its possible dimensions (individual, collective, institutional, national, and disciplinary conditions).

2.4.1 Scientific Journals and Scientific Articles

The main role of scientists is to develop new knowledge and, in order to effectively contribute to science, it should be released in such a way that other scientists can understand and assess it (Pires-Noronha & Aguilar-Población, 2002). Scientific journals and scientific articles are the most important media for scientific communication and are fundamental for the certification, quality control, and visibility of knowledge, considering that scientists widely resort to them (Miguel, Gómez, & Bongiovani, 2012).

The United Nations Educational, Scientific and Cultural Organization (UNESCO, 2002) defines scientific journals as periodical publications that offer especially scientific articles, which are written by different authors and contain current information on the research and development of any scientific field. Journals have a distinctive name, they are published at regular intervals, usually several times a year, and each issue is consecutively numbered or dated. Its basic component, the scientific article, is written in prose and it is published as a contribution to the progress of science.

The American Library Association (ALA, 2011) offers another view of scientific journals, which emphasizes that they include original articles on the research and development of a particular field of science, which makes them researchers' medium of choice to communicate the first writing about their results, considering that articles' contents represent a contribution to knowledge.

Considering the scientific journal as the most viable medium to communicate research findings is justified by their role in combining interventions and innovations, something that researchers highly seek in order to track the progress of science. This type of information source originated in scientific communities, but there was an increase in the publication of journals by other institutions such as universities, research institutions, government agencies, and private publishers (Abadal-Falgueras & Ruis-Alcaraz, 2006). Moreover, because scientific journals are the main source for scientific communication, they provide a comprehensive contribution to the development of science from the role they play in circulating research results (Marca-Altamirano, 2011; Villamón-Herrera, Devís-Devís, Valencia-Peris, & Valenciano-Valcárcel, 2007).

Scientific journals show particular characteristics: each has its own distinct identity which is defined through its objectives and thematic scope, its patterns for acceptance regarding authorship, content type, and extension, as well as references and style (Franco-Paredes, Díaz-Reséndiz, Pineda-Lozano, & Hidalgo-Rasmussen, 2016). Such identification indicators are grouped as follows: (1) those related to formal aspects, taking into consideration the choice of a style manual for formatting and presenting documents; (2) specific aspects of content and structure; and (3) those elements that define their quality levels through the impact of the journal within its field (Abadal-Falgueras & Ruis-Alcaraz, 2006).

With Open Access (OA) initiatives, scientific journals and also books have undergone a radical change regarding their publication, distribution, and use of their contents. A clear example of OA and the incorporation of ICT in scientific communication has occurred with the use of the Free Online Scholarship (FOS) and the Open Journal System (OJS) (Pires-Noronha & Aguiar-Población, 2002). To avoid volatility and to ensure the permanence of digital publications, scientific publishers have incorporated the use of an alphanumeric code known as Digital Object Identifer (DOI).

A first classification of scientific journals can be established from the perspective of their publication and access models: (1) OA journals: offering access at no cost to the full-text documents, either immediately or after a period of embargo has passed; (2) subscription journals offering the possibility of self-archive: which brings the possibility of generating and sharing OA versions of the published articles, but this will depend on whether the authors can assume the work involved in self-archiving, once the publisher's license agreement allows it. It is possible to subdivide this category into another two according to the OA policy, green journals allow self-archiving of an author's version after an embargo period has passed and yellow journals allow to make the published version OA after the payment of an Article Processing Charge (APC) to the publisher; (3) journals without OA possibilities: these prohibit self-archiving and their access is offered only through individual or institutional subscriptions (Abadal-Falgueras & Ruis-Alcaraz, 2006).

From the perspective of the publishing entities, scientific journals can be classified into three types: (1) first level: published and edited by internationally recognized scientific societies, they are regularly inexpensive and supported by its members; (2) second level: the editing, publishing, distribution, and marketing are done through large multinational companies, but their high cost may limit their circulation; (3) third level: journals published by universities, research centers, hospitals, and other knowledge institutions, they have some challenges regarding editing, low operating budgets and hence of copies, little presence in scientific indexes, and their publication periods as well as their distribution and dissemination are generally irregular. Another classification of scientific journals is according to the types of contributions they receive: (1) informational: which disseminate programs of scientific, technical, and educational nature; (2) primary: they publish original scientific articles; (3) secondary: they include only summaries of primary sources; and (4) tertiary: they publish scientific and technological advances (López-Ornelas & Cordero-Arroyo, 2005).

The scientific article is a written report containing original research results and it becomes a valid publication or a primary scientific publication if its contents are clear and systematic enough that it allows to assess authors' observations, repeat their experiments, and evaluate their intellectual processes (Mendoza & Paravic, 2006; Samar & Ávila, 2004).

In relation to the contents and purposes of the scientific articles, they can be classified into two types: *review article*, with theoretical-philosophical contents that are composed of general or theoretical scientific concepts, with scientific knowledge explanations or explorations; and *scientific article*, which includes factual information supported by experimental evidence, as well as observations and generalizations. Both types integrate theoretical and practical-methodological work using the scientific method. Some scientific journals offer the possibility of publishing other minor article genres, such as editorials, letters to the editor, opinion columns (that despite their more free nature, tend to be scientifically grounded), book reviews of publications considered of interest to readers, and brief reports of case studies or research drafts.

Depending on their quality, scientific articles could be accepted in various scientific journals, which can also be classified by quality levels. The quality of journals will make some more demanding than others and this is what will determine the extension and level of complexity that an article must have in order to be published in the journal the researcher wants to publish in. The classification of scientific journals according to their level of quality, visibility, and impact is the following: (1) journals of excellence: integrated by journals with the highest impact factor, positioned in the first quartile of international citation rankings of their field in the Journal Citation Reports, which are available through Web of Science; (2) Category A journals: international scientific journals of the highest level and prestige, especially those included in the scientific databases and Web of Science, they are within quartiles two to four; (3) Category B journals: quality scientific journals without sufficient internationalization levels. Although they have publishing standards and are cited to some extent, they are not indexed by Web of Science, but they are in other recognized systems such as Scopus or SCImago; (4) Category C journals: scientific journals that are considered of second order, they have low citations, they may be international journals but they are less relevant and they are indexed in general distribution lists such as Latindex or Redalyc and in scientific databases of the aggregator type such as EBSCO and ProQuest, which index multiple publishers; and (5) Category D journals: all publications not included in the above categories, they have dubious scientific status, are not indexed in any distribution list, nor in any scientific database of medium or high scientific recognition (Torres-Salinas et al., 2010). The latter category includes journals of very low circulation and that are not usually indexed, the so-called predatory journals may be included as well.

Internationally, scientific journals are grouped into two types according to their levels of quality and influence: mainstream and peripheral journals, and they have varied levels of requirements regarding the scientific and research rigor of their published contents (Núñez-Jover, 2006). The journals regularly considered mainstream are only those included in Web of Science's indexes (Science Citation Index and Social Science Citation Index), while the rest are considered peripheral.

However, peripheral journals are often defended with the argument that many offer substantial contents and follow similar manuscript selection processes as those in the mainstream. They are not included in Web of Science but they are included in others that are also important (e.g., Scopus), they have a broad coverage regarding their content, they use infometric indicators to show their high quality, such as the score that is calculated in Scopus' SCImago Journal Rank (SJR), number of citations or the immediacy index; although some do not do any of this. Additionally, journals and publishers have begun to consider Altmetrics as other quality indicators.

The study of peripheral scientific journals has gained importance, as these are considered essential in the development of regional science of developing countries, they are also in constant struggles for achieving higher levels and reaching the mainstream, so they are careful in complying with difficult issues such as: continuity (being published at regular intervals), strict peer review, and the availability of sufficient articles for publication (Ríos-Ortega, 2006). If researchers either seek to only publish in mainstream journals or only in peripheral magazines, both are equally wrong perspectives. A balanced scientific communication must consider both types, since researchers have to take into account that they must: (1) ensure the access and distribution of scientific production within and for the institutions in their own environments, regardless of those budget issues that may prevent many institutions from access to the acquisition of mainstream journals' subscriptions; that is why publishing in peripheral journals can ensure that their findings reach a wider audience; (2) consider distribution channels within scientific communities around the world, for the reason mentioned above; and (3) consider that the OA model used by many peripheral journals for their distribution allows a greater number of researchers to have access to scientific knowledge. For this reason, it is also important that, if the author publishes in a "green" OA journal, even if it is mainstream, they have to assume its responsibility of self-archiving an OA version of their article and preferably in a repository, whether institutional, national, or disciplinary.

According to the different classifications of scientific journals described above, in conclusion, it is possible to group them into three kinds: (1) indexed journals: they have an editorial board of recognized members within their discipline; they are included in international indexes where infometric analyses are prepared and the journals that will be especially valued are those having an impact factor and therefore indexed in Web of Science. However, other indexes are also considered valid, such as: Scopus, Inspec, SciVal, SCImago, PubMed, Academic OneFile, ACM Digital Library, LISTA, PsycINFO, DOAJ, CrossRef, Astrophysics Data Sistem, Parity Computing, and Google Scholar; (2) refereed journals: they have an editorial evaluation system generally less strict that those in the indexed journals and are included in the above-cited indexes, except in Web of Science; and (3) dissemination journals: they are intended for a large audience, include general themes, and their texts have a generally accessible language (see Section 2.3.5).

2.4.2 Scientific Books

The book or monograph is defined as a document that results from a finished investigation, generally documental, which analyzes, synthesizes, and integrates the results of published research, mainly scientific articles, other books, and theses. The scientific book deals with a specific topic within a scientific, technological, or humanistic field, or they are about different historical, psychological, or sociological phenomena (Corona-Lisboa, 2015).

The content of the scientific book provides a description, narration, or explanatory exposition on a given topic within a scientific discipline. The content must be original, both on the basis of the sources used and their analysis, but it should also address its topics in depth (Ejarque, 2005). As with other scientific products, scientific books can be presented in different formats: printed, digital (e-book), or both.

Monographs are classified into two types: (1) authored book: integrating contents that were developed by one or more persons that are experts on the subject in question, and its content are attributed to these authors; and (2) compiled or edited book: monographs that gather previously published or unpublished texts (chapters) written by several authors on a given topic; they are not intended to create new knowledge, but to help in the scientific communication and dissemination of a particular subject. The possible roles it entails are: editor, compiler, or coordinator, as well as chapter authors.

After the publication of a scientific article, the edition, coordination, or compiling of a book is the most important activity within the range of quality recognitions regarding scientific communication that a researcher can obtain. Authored books have a higher value when compared to edited books, given the intellectual effort required to develop contents by one or more authors against the efforts involving the compilation of book chapters that were the responsibility of different authors. In addition, editors can display different commitment levels regarding the compiled book, which is an element not measured, and therefore editors could dedicate much, little, or no effort to the review and quality control of the selected chapters during their publication.

2.4.3 Book Chapters

Book chapters are the most important division of a monograph, as it is a fragmentation made for facilitating its readability and optimizing the organization and integration of its contents. Each chapter is a part or section within a given work and its extension may vary, depending on the intentions and needs of the author, as well as those of the subject studied.

Book chapters represent a normal separation in the case of authored books. However, in edited books, they represent an independent unit, both in content and authorship (each has its own authorship) and, as a whole, all chapters constitute the edited book. Regarding the evaluation of scientific communication, the authorship of a book chapter has more value than the participation as an editor, since the latter represents a lower intellectual challenge.

2.4.4 Theses

Theses are key products within scientific communication processes, and their importance lies in various aspects, such as: (1) they are the first formal research work of students in all academic levels, therefore the professional preparation of a graduate from a higher education institution that does not include its presentation as a mandatory requirement for graduation is considered poor; (2) they constitute an efficient way to provide research training for new human resources and for promoting a scientific culture; (3) they count with the leadership and the validation of a senior researcher who supervises and accompanies the student in its development, although sometimes this is not a guarantee of a thesis' quality; and (4) they represent a research result that enables deriving other scientific products that can give visibility to the research findings during the thesis' preparation period and after its delivery, such as scientific articles, books, book chapters, or conference presentations.

Theses present research processes conducted by the candidates to earn academic degrees. Their contents are usually characterized by including a theoretical framework, the problem statement, a methodology for studying it and the scientific results of a field study. These contents must be presented in a systematic, logical, and objective manner, while offering solutions to a problem posed that are guided by the scientific method. A thesis presents conclusions, proposals, opinions, or theories about a specific problem; it is work of a scientific nature and must include a concrete and specific contribution to solving a particular problem.

Because of their research nature, theses are considered scientific documents, and are subject to a special set of rules, which include submitting original conclusions, adhering to facts and not opinions, and the application of a scientific methodology. The fulfillment of the above aspects grants the thesis with a key educational level that is recognized by a scientific community and it contributes to academic production, becoming a highly influential element from an educational perspective. It should be noted that theses are considered gray literature, although they truly feed scientific dissemination actions, they do not contribute to scientific communication, unless other specific products are derived from them. It is also important to consider that gray literature refers to documents of limited circulation, which are not usually available through conventional channels. This greatly complicates their acquisition and therefore, their visibility. Gray literature usually lacks standardized numbers (ISBN, ISSN, official identification numbers, or legal deposit) and are not supported by a publisher. However, universities with a high level of progress will prioritize theses' development and dissemination as well as research in general as institutional priorities. Such universities will perform some or all of the following activities regarding theses, either in coordination with the students or on their behalf: obtaining a standardized number for the monograph, print copies under the university publishing, and the deposit of a digital version in an institutional or national repository.

Theses contributions to scientific production and education processes will occur if the following considerations are met: (1) they provide a long-term useful contribution thanks to the use of repositories or any other means to facilitate their visibility and access; (2) they are essential for the functioning of universities and research institutions; (3) they are elements of significant influence in the educational processes of developing social and intellectual capital, both within the institutions and for the training of human resources in research.

2.4.5 Patents

These are generally defined as an exclusive right granted to individuals or institutions on the detailed description of the construction or operation of an invention, a product, or process, as well as its usage. They provide a new way of doing something or a new way to technically solve a problem. Patents are mainly framed within the rules and regulations defined in each country regarding industrial and intellectual property. This kind of scientific document has two distinctive features that are common to other scientific documents that conform to scientific communication: they represent the clearer example of innovation processes in knowledge institutions; and they are not typically developed in every scientific discipline, just in those related to technological innovation.

Patents are a peculiar document within scientific communication, because they do not occur with the same frequency in a given period as scientific articles. The main features that differentiate them from other scientific documents are: (1) the author has a high level of exclusivity in their use, possession, benefits, and rights of action (exclusive rights), notably the rights to its economic exploitation, a crucial difference next to scientific articles, which do not report any direct financial gains; (2) their obsolescence is defined by their lifespan (unless otherwise indicated, it depends on the applicable laws, the type of patent, and the country it was registered in), however, its lifespan is broader than any other scientific document; (3) although scientific knowledge has a global sense, in the case of patents, space limitations are defined and they may be subject to national and international legislation.

The importance of patent development within the scientific communication at knowledge institutions, lies in several aspects: (1) they can generate economic benefits to authors; (2) given the above aspect, they encourage creativity and innovation; (3) their contents have broad legal protections; (4) patents are a scientific product that contributes to the development of knowledge institutions, and they reflect the scientific conditions of a country in a direct relation with the sectors of economic and social development.

2.4.6 Conference Proceedings

This type of scientific document is preceded by a presentation in an academic event, regularly known as a congress, conference, or symposium, which requires authors to submit a full text related to their presentation. The results of these events are regularly integrated into a monograph, which compiles a selection of these full texts and in some cases involves the peer review of such texts. According to the vision of academics and institutions dedicated to the evaluation of scientific production, conference proceedings are not always considered as part of scientific communication, instead they are considered to be within scientific dissemination, as their evaluation and edition processes are not usually deemed rigorous enough. However, some established conferences that publish their proceedings under academic publishers include strict peer review, the work of editors and style reviewers, and they are indexed in Scopus and even in Web of Science's Conference Proceedings Citation Index; although the latter does not include the calculation of an impact factor for the conference proceedings it indexes, unlike its other citation indexes.

Both the participation in conferences, as well as the inclusion of a full text in the conference proceedings, are widely valued in academic and scientific environments, since they are considered to be an indicator of scientific impact, especially in medical disciplines. Furthermore, they allow evaluating the capabilities a researcher has for appearing and presenting in public, which involve possessing self-confidence, effective time management, appropriate oratory and rhetoric skills, and even having the possibility of disseminating their research findings in more than one language. The main objectives of communicating scientific findings in conferences are: (1) exchange knowledge directly; (2) participate in an educational setting for training new generations; (3) stimulating professional development; (4) conduct a motivational function; and (5) a social function, through the socialization among professionals (Betlloch-Mas, Silvestre-Salvador, & Belinchón-Romero, 2009). Conferences also allow the researcher to expand their networks of professional contacts and collaborators.

2.4.7 Scientific Databases

Scientific databases are validation instruments for new paradigms of scientific communication. They allow measuring with bibliometric indicators to define the productivity or collaboration of authors, disciplines, institutions, and countries, according to the patterns and structures of their scientific publication (Mugnaini, 2006).

Although databases are not documents that may be considered within scientific communication functions for themselves, they become instruments for scientific communication, dissemination, and development. They can be considered a secondary source that facilitates access to primary documents (including scientific articles and other scientific products, depending on the database) for generating new products. The greater the prestige and recognition scientific journals have, the more likely that they are indexed in the main databases, which facilitate their location, consultation, and retrieval through various access points and the metadata of their contents: title, authors, institutional affiliation, countries, publication name and its identification details, abstract, keywords, and even full text. The precision and quality of their records as well as the explicit presentation of the different access points, will contribute to a greater visibility for its contents, both individually in a given database or globally through meta search engines or discovery services.

Scientific databases or indexing systems are spaces that store the digital information that resulted from scientific production. These devices allow assessing scientific communication results from authors and even institutions, countries, and disciplines. Their logical and disciplinary organization systems allow retrieving large amounts of documents with precision, thus facilitating their citation. Scientific databases are classified into two groups:

1. *Commercial databases*: these include scientific papers published in the most prestigious journals that correspond to the mainstream, their use represents a high cost, the contents are preponderantly provided in English and knowledge institutions acquired them as information services. These can be subdivided into three types: (1) Scientific publishers databases: offered by the major scientific commercial publishers and provide only content published by them, these databases include Elsevier's ScienceDirect, Springer-Nature's SpringerLink, Wiley-Blackwell, Taylor & Francis, SAGE Publishing, and Emerald Insight; (2) Aggregators: these group in subject-specific packages several publications of different publishers, which can be consulted with full-text access or only at a reference level according to each publisher's different access conditions and licenses. The aggregator databases are offered by the two main current competitors: EBSCO Information Services and ProQuest; (3) Indices: these contain only reference data from most of the mainstream publications and are central in the evaluation processes of scientific production. The most important are Scopus and Web of Science.
2. *OA databases*: these include peer-reviewed scientific articles from journals that, although peripheral, offer high-quality contents with free access. OA databases can fulfill both functions as indexes and aggregators, some examples are SCImago, DOAJ, SciELO, Internet Archive, Europeana, and Redalyc; which can also be classified as repositories.

2.4.8 Institutional Repositories

Repositories are OA platforms that offer access to their contents at no cost to users, mainly they can be classified into three types: (1) institutional, which are limited to a single knowledge institution and self-archiving involves the institution's departments and researchers; (2) regional, these exclusively integrate a selection of journals published within a given region in one place, they do not offer the possibility of self-archiving for authors;. and (3) worldwide disciplinary, which gather the production or a given field of knowledge and support self-archiving by researchers from any country. Institutional and worldwide disciplinary repositories are powered by researchers who assume the self-archiving of their own scientific production, including in many cases the OA versions of the publications they made in journals that support self-archiving under certain conditions.

Although all three types of repositories are valuable for scientific communication and dissemination, this section focuses on institutional repositories, as they are perhaps the most important for the scientific production evaluation of researchers, institutions, and countries. Considering that current knowledge institutions generate diverse contents within their sphere of productivity, which are not always considered scientific communication but dissemination, there is the emergent need to make contents available to the largest amount of people possible. This need is met through institutional repositories.

An institutional repository is a digital platform that gathers a set of documents collected by using international standards of organization, metadata description, and interoperability that are typical of the OA movement, and these documents are either digitized or digital-born (Silva & Tomaél, 2011). These kinds of knowledge dissemination services are originated through the individual initiative of a knowledge institution that has reached a level of maturity characterized by an awareness of the value of preserving and disseminating their scientific production and the wish to increase its international visibility. Therefore, an institutional repository is a voluntary initiative which is supported by the institutions' infrastructure and resources.

Institutional repositories are information systems that collect, preserve, disseminate, and provide access to the intellectual, scientific, and academic production of university communities; thus becoming a key element for teaching and research, which also allow to: (1) maximize the visibility, use, and impact of the scientific and academic production; (2) provide feedback to research and encourage it; (3) produce, support, and improve the quality and value of institutional publications; and (4) facilitate access to the academic information that is not considered part of the scientific communication (Bustos-González, Fernández-Porcel, & Johnson, 2007). If institutional repositories are developed appropriately and according to international standards of organization and interoperability, their contents will be easily indexed in national and disciplinary-global repositories, as well as gaining an impressive boost in visibility after they are indexed by Google Scholar.

Sometimes, institutional repositories are created in order to expand the information and knowledge available in all sectors of society. In addition, they allow solving the institutional problem of not having a formal access channel to its own production, when an institution does not have any form of systematic organization for documents produced within it. Therefore, the production disseminated through institutional repositories becomes products typical of scientific communication.

From the perspective of their contribution to scientific dissemination, measuring the effectiveness of institutional repositories consists of the following key indicators: (1) the identification of institutional policies to determine the appropriate documentary objects to be included or excluded in the repository (in some cases the academic production will be included); (2) the institutional planning mechanisms for valuing and supporting this information service; (3) digitization procedures and the conversion to new formats for the oldest documents; (4) the identification of a method for defining the organization of different schemes for grouping documents; (5) the possibilities of connectivity and interoperability with other repositories, as well as establishing hyperlinks and policies for providing full-text access to documents; and (6) the definition of marketing projects and preservation strategies (Westell, 2006).

Unlike the scientific communication measurement processes through scientific databases, institutional repositories do not really offer accurate procedures for measuring their impact, since this is not necessarily their intention. However, recent initiatives include the integration of a combination of infometric indicators and Altmetrics to measure the impact of repositories. Nevertheless, repositories' basic function is considered to be that of preserving institutional documents, as the quintessential way of preserving institutional memory and of contributing to the development of scientific and academic productivity environments.

2.5 FEATURES AND QUALITY LEVELS OF SCIENTIFIC COMMUNICATION

According to the perspective of each analysis, the quality measurement of scientific communication has multiple variables, which can range from recording the amount of products to analyzing their internal consistency or measuring their impact through citations, metrics, and their influence on society. Regardless of the approach, it is necessary to generate measurement indicators that allow identifying different levels, characteristics, and conditions of scientific production.

A measurement model for quality assessment with a global perspective contains three dimensions: (1) indicators by nature: including infometric indicators, which measure the academic attention toward a given scientific document and Altmetrics, which measure attention at a broader level; (2) indicators by type: organizational, thematic, and by number of publications; and (3) indicators by level: micro, meso, and macro. The influence of scientific communication indicators includes: (1) collective action, when research groups, educational bodies, institutions, countries, or publications are evaluated; and, (2) individually, consisting of researcher-level or article-level evaluations (Igami, 2011). Other elements may also be considered as the identification of concrete actions taken in order to encourage the creation of new knowledge, the extent to which certain researchers and scientific communities collaborate, and even the number of meetings that took place for facilitating intellectual exchange (Bosch, 2011).

From the perspective and impact of the products that were scientifically communicated, the most widely used vision for measuring scientific quality is based on the integration of traditional metric indicators, which are part of the following disciplines: (1) Bibliometrics: these measure the internal consistency of documents according to the obsolescence levels of the references they contain or identifying publications' half-lives; (2) Infometrics: uses citations records for generating indicators such as impact factor, immediacy index, or the Hirsch index, among others (González-Nando, 2007); and (3) Scientometrics: this involves conducting measurements over scientific communication's socioeconomic influence in investment projects, improvement in gross domestic product, or in determining the benefits implied in the commercialization of scientific products when they are treated as interchangeable goods (Morales-Campos & Martínez-Arellano, 2011).

Metric studies of information have different applications across all the products that conform scientific communication, but they really take an approach that exclusively measures the quality of the scientific journals and the publications where such products are included. Hence, individual documents must also be evaluated considering their separate citation behavior. Measuring scientific journals' quality can be done in two fundamental ways: (1) by their endogenous behavior using bibliometrics, which is based on the consistency of the documents from the perspective of their levels of obsolescence; and (2) by their exogenous behavior using infometrics, from the impact that each document has according to its impact pattern and citations (Gorbea-Portal, 2004). It should be noted that scientific articles are accepted or rejected according to their quality and originality, which are aspects that are evaluated during double-blind peer-review process. Despite being criticized by the scientific community, mainly due to objectivity concerns, this kind of evaluation process functions as the best way to certify, validate, and ensure the quality of scientific journals' contents (Márquez-Jiménez, 2014; Romanos de Tiratel et al., 2010).

The scientific content of published articles is considered of quality as they have been evaluated under rigorous selection according to the journal's own level of quality, and are grouped by nuclei (mainstream or peripheral journals), subgroup (indexed, peer-review, dissemination), and by specific criteria (impact factor level, location by quartile, obsolescence, or half-life). Rozemblum, Unzurrunzaga, Banzato, and Pucacco (2015) identify two concepts for scientific communication measurement: (1) scientific quality: studied according to the peer-review evaluation procedure and the originality of the content as perceived by the members of scientific communities; and (2) editorial quality: constituted by contextual and formal elements of the journal that, although they should not be above the level of the contents, are still important.

As a conclusion, the main parameter for measuring science and its communication consists in determining its benefits for society in general. UNESCO's (2000) perspective is "science in the service of knowledge; knowledge in the service of progress." This recognizes scientific work as a function that systematically and exhaustively studies research findings to generate new knowledge. Knowledge catalysts are the national policies that facilitate the activities and communication among scientific knowledge actors; who must have a social purpose, which will be fulfilled through the development of social and technological goods that can ultimately favor all citizens.

REFERENCES

Abadal-Falgueras, E., & Ruis-Alcaraz, L. (2006). Revistas científicas digitales: características e indicadores. *Revista de Universidad y Sociedad del Conocimiento, 3*(1), 6–20. <http://www.uoc.edu/rusc/3/1/dt/esp/abadal_rius.pdf> Accessed 16.08.09.

Alarcó-Hernández, A. (1999). *Periodismo científico en la prensa diaria: Aspectos de biomedicina* (PhD Thesis). España: Universidad de la Laguna. <ftp://tesis.bbtk.ull.es/ccssyhum/cs80.pdf> Accessed 16.08.09.

Albornoz, M. (2007). Los problemas de la ciencia y el poder. *Revista Iberoamericana de Ciencia, Tecnología y Sociedad - CTS, 3*(8), 47–65. <http://www.redalyc.org/pdf/924/92430805.pdf> Accessed 16.08.09.

Alcántara, L. (2009). *Not just talk: Individual and institutional critical factors affecting knowledge production from systematic cooperative inquiry groups. (PhD Thesis).* USA: Teachers College, Columbia University. <http://search.proquest.com/docview/304865019> Accessed 16.08.09.

Alli, A. (2002). *The effects academic origin and academic affiliation on research productivity: An empirical investigation of information systems faculty. (PhD Thesis).* USA: Mississippi State University.

Altamirano-Sánchez, M. (2006). Distribución social del conocimiento: Estrategia de comunicación universitaria para el desarrollo sostenible. In: *I Congreso Iberoamericano de Ciencia, Tecnología, Sociedad e Innovación CTS + 1.* Mexico, D.F., Mexico. <www.oei.es/memoriasctsi/mesa16/m16p02.pdf> Accessed 16.08.09.

American Library Association. (2011). <http://www.ala.org> Accessed 16.08.09.

Avogadro, M. (2002). Periodismo científico: Un puente entre las personas y el universo científico-cultural. *Razón y Palabra, 30.* <http://www.razonypalabra.org.mx/comunicarte/2002/diciembre.html> Accessed 16.08.09.

Bailey, T. (1992). *A study of faculty research productivity.* (PhD Thesis). USA: University of Virginia, Curry School of Education.

Badley, G. (2002). A really useful link between teaching and research. *Teaching in Higher Education,* 7(4), 443–455. Available from http://dx.doi.org/10.1080/135625102760553937.

Banús, E. (2006). La estrategia de redes de conocimiento adoptada por la UNESCO. In M. Albornoz, & C. Alfaraz (Eds.), *Redes de conocimiento: Construcción dinámica y gestión* (pp. 11–14). Buenos Aires, Argentina: Red Iberoamericana de Indicadores de Ciencia y Tecnología (RICYT). <http://www.ricyt.org/manuales/doc_view/26-redes-de-conocimiento-construccion-dinamica-y-gestion> Accessed 16.08.09.

Belenguer-Jané, M. (2002). Geografía y viajes en el periodismo científico. *Comunicar, 9*(19), 55–59. <http://www.revistacomunicar.com/verpdf.php?numero=19&articulo=19-2002-10> Accessed 16.08.09.

Berger, P., & Luckmann, T. (2001). *La construcción social de la realidad.* Buenos Aires, Argentina: Amorrortu.

Betlloch-Mas, I., Silvestre-Salvador, J., & Belinchón-Romero, I. (2009). ¿Se debe medir la calidad científica de un congreso nacional por el porcentaje de comunicaciones que llegan a publicarse? *Actas Dermo-Sifiliográficas, 100*(7), 635–636. Available from http://dx.doi.org/10.1016/S0001-7310(09)71922-2.

Beyer-Ruiz, M., & Hernández-García, C. (2009). La divulgación de la ciencia. In *La enciclopedia de las Ciencias y la Tecnología en México.* <http://www.izt.uam.mx/cosmosecm/DIVULGACION_DE_LAS_CIENCIAS.html> Accessed 16.08.09.

Bland, C., Center, B., Finstad, D., & Risbey, K. (2005). A theoretical, practical, predictive model of faculty and department research productivity. *Academic Medicine, 80*(3), 225–237. Available from http://dx.doi.org/10.1097/00001888-200503000-00006.

Boardman, P. (2006). *University research center and the composition of academic work. (PhD thesis).* USA: Georgia Institute of Technology.

Bosch, M. (2011). *Dimensión ética de la comunicación científica y tecnológica.* Buenos Aires, Argentina: Instituto Nacional de Tecnología Agropecuaria, Gerencia del Sistema de Información y Comunicación.

Braga, C., Bernardete, M., & Silva, M. (2003). Errores en las referencias bibliográficas de la producción académica: Un estudio de caso. *Scire, 9*(1), 133–138. <http://www.ibersid.eu/ojs/index.php/scire/article/view/1461/1439> Accessed 16.08.09.

Brew, A. (2003). Teaching and research: New relationships and their implications for inquiry-based teaching and learning in higher education. *Higher Education Research &*

Development, *22*(1), 3–18. Available from http://dx.doi.org/10.1080/07294360320000056571.

Brown, R., & McCartney, S. (1998). The link between research and teaching: Its purpose and implications. *Innovations in Education and Training International*, *35*(2), 117–129. Available from http://dx.doi.org/10.1080/1355800980350205.

Bustos, B. (2010). *Geographies of knowledge production in a neoliberal setting: The case of Los Lagos region, Chile. (PhD thesis).* USA: Syracuse University.

Bustos-González, A., Fernández-Porcel, A., & Johnson, I. (2007). Guidelines for the creation of institutional repositories at universities and higher education institutions. Brussels, Belgium: European Commission. <http://eprints.rclis.org/13512/> Accessed 16.08.09.

Bustos-Mora, G. (2004). Ciencia y tecnología en la prensa escrita costarricense: Análisis de casos. *Revista de Ciencias Sociales*, *4*(106), 215–229. <http://www.redalyc.org/articulo.oa?id = 15310616> Accessed 16.08.09.

Calvo-Hernando, M. (2001). *Divulgación y periodismo científico: Entre la claridad y la exactitud.* Mexico, D.F., Mexico: Universidad Nacional Autónoma de México, Dirección General de Divulgación de la Ciencia.

Campos-Rosas, J. (2000). La comunicación científica: ¿Arte o ciencia? *Ars Pharmaceutica*, *41*(1), 11–18. <http://farmacia.ugr.es/ars/pdf/177.pdf> Accessed 16.08.09.

Canales, A., & Luna, E. (2003). ¿Cuál política para la docencia? *Revista de la Educación Superior*, *32*(127), 45–52. <http://publicaciones.anuies.mx/pdfs/revista/Revista127_S3A2ES.pdf> Accessed 16.08.09.

Chauí, M. (2001). *Escritos sobre a universidade.* São Paulo, Brazil: Editora da Universidad Estatal Paulista.

Corona-Lisboa, J. (2015). Uso e importancia de las monografías. *Revista Cubana de Investigaciones Biomédicas*, *34*(1), 64–68. <http://scielo.sld.cu/pdf/ibi/v34n1/ibi07115.pdf> Accessed 16.08.09.

Crosta, P., & Packman, I. (2005). Faculty productivity in supervising doctoral students' dissertations at Cornell University. *Economics of Education Review*, *24*(1), 55–65. Available from http://dx.doi.org/10.1016/j.econedurev.2004.03.011.

Daza, T., & Aroleda, T. (2007). Comunicación pública de la ciencia y la tecnología en Colombia: ¿Políticas para la democratización del conocimiento? *Signo y Pensamiento*, *26*(50), 100–125. <http://www.redalyc.org/articulo.oa?id=86005008> Accessed 16.08.09.

Díaz-Barriga, F., & Rigo, M. (2003). Realidades y paradigmas de la función docente: Implicaciones sobre la evaluación magisterial en educación superior. *Revista de la Educación Superior*, *32*(127), 53–61. <http://publicaciones.anuies.mx/pdfs/revista/Revista127_S3A3ES.pdf> Accessed 16.08.09.

Doellefeld, S. (1998). *Faculty productivity: A conceptual analysis and research synthesis.* (PhD Thesis). USA: State University of New York.

Ejarque, D. (2005). La monografía. In L. Cubo de Severino (Ed.), *Los textos de la ciencia: Principales clases del discurso académico – científico* (pp. 221–234). Córdoba, Argentina: Comunicarte Editorial.

Elton, L. (2001). Research and teaching: Conditions for a positive link. *Teaching in Higher Education*, *6*(1), 43–56. Available from http://dx.doi.org/10.1080/13562510020029590.

Erazo-Pesántez, M. (2009). *La comunicación pública de la ciencia en el centro de la política científica. (PhD Thesis).* Spain: Universidad de Salamanca.

Feldmann, M. (2005). *Do congressional Academic earmarks at public research encourage research productivity? (PhD thesis).* USA: Iowa State University.

Fernández-Aquino, O., & Valdés-Puentes, R. (2008). Formación docente y trabajo metodológico en la universidad: Resultados de una experiencia de desarrollo profesional centrada en la reflexión, el apoyo mutuo y la supervision. *Pro-Posições*, *19*(1), 75–95. <http://www.scielo.br/pdf/pp/v19n1/a13v19n1.pdf> Accessed 16.08.09.

Franco-Paredes, K., Díaz-Reséndiz, F., Pineda-Lozano, E., & Hidalgo-Rasmussen, C. (2016). Bibliometric analysis of scientific production of Mexican journal of eating disorders, 2010-2014. *Revista Mexicana de Trastornos Alimentarios*, 7(1), 9–16. Available from http://dx.doi.org/10.1016/j.rmta.2016.03.001.

Fushimi, M., Mallo, J., & Pichinini, M. (2005). *Memoria académica y científica: El rol de la biblioteca universitaria en la preservación y difusión generado en las universidades. Cuartas Jornadas de Sociología de la UNLP: La Argentina de la Crisis*. La Plata, Argentina: Universidad Nacional de la Plata, Facultad de Humanidades y Ciencias de la Educación. <http://eprints.rclis.org/9879> Accessed 16.08.09.

García-Cepero, M. (2007). *Institutional and individual factors associated with faculty scholarly productivity. (PhD thesis)*. USA: University of Connecticut.

Gonzalez-Argote, J., Garcia-Rivero, A., & Dorta-Contreras, A. (2016). Producción científica estudiantil en revistas médicas cubanas 1995-2014: Primera etapa. *Investigación en Educación Médica, 5*(19), 155–163. Available from http://dx.doi.org/10.1016/j.riem.2016.01.023.

González-Nando, E. (2007). *La investigación científica en la Universidad Nacional Autónoma de México: Un perfil bibliométrico*. (PhD thesis). España: Universidad de Murcia. <https://digitum.um.es/xmlui/handle/10201/153> Accessed 16.08.09.

Gorbea-Portal, S. (2004). *Producción y comunicación científica latinoamericana en ciencias bibliotecológicas y de la información. (PhD Thesis)*. Madrid, Spain: Universidad Carlos III de Madrid.

Gutiérrez-Couto, U., Blanco-Pérez, A., & Casal-Acción, B. (2004). Cómo realizar una comunicación científica: Estructura de la comunicación científica. *Revista Gallega de Terapia Ocupacional TOG*, (1), 1–17. <http://eprints.rclis.org/10377/> Accessed 16.08.09.

Gutiérrez-Vargas, M. (2002). El aprendizaje de la ciencia y de la información científica en la educación superior. *Anales de Documentación*, (5), 197–212. <http://www.redalyc.org/articulo.oa?id = 63500507> Accessed 16.08.09.

Hernández-Castañón, M., García-Valenzuela, M., Uicab-Pool, G., Calini, M., & Mendes, I. (2008). Barreras y estrategias para la divulgación de conocimiento de enfermería en México. *Desarrollo Científico de Enfermería, 16*(10), 429–433. <http://www.index-f.com/dce/16/r16-429.php> Accessed 16.08.09.

Hernández-Gutiérrez, P. (2014). *Métrica de la producción científica en universidades públicas estales mexicanas*. (PhD thesis). Chihuahua. Mexico: Universidad Autónoma de Chihuahua.

Herrera-Lima, S. (2007). *La profesionalización de la comunicación pública de la ciencia: Hacia la construcción de un campo académico*. <www.redpop.org/wp-content/uploads/2015/06/susanaherrera.doc> Accessed 16.08.09.

Howell, S. (2000). *Work teams, knowledge production and learning: A critical analysis of quality improvement processes. (PhD thesis)*. PA, USA: Pennsylvania State University, College of Education.

Igami, M. (2011). *Elaboração de indicadores de produção científica com base na análise cienciométrica das dissertações e teses do IPEN. (PhD thesis)*. São Paulo, Brazil: Instituto de Pesquisas Energeticas e Nucleares. <http://www.teses.usp.br/teses/disponiveis/85/85134/tde-15092011-150503/pt-br.php> Accessed 16.08.09.

Izquierdo-Alonso, M., Moreno-Fernández, L., & Izquierdo-Arroyo, J. (2008). Grupos de investigación en contextos organizacionales académicos: Una reflexión sobre los procesos de cambio y los retos futuros. *Investigación Bibliotecológica, 22*(44), 103–141. <http://www.scielo.org.mx/pdf/ib/v22n44/v22n44a7.pdf> Accessed 16.08.09.

Jennings, J. (1997). *Faculty productivity: A contemporary analysis of faculty perspectives*. (PhD thesis). Stanford, USA: Stanford University, School of Education.

Jiménez, E., Rangel, P., & Albornoz, O. (2004). *Invención, innovación y difusión del conocimiento: La producción académica en Venezuela*. In: II Seminario Internacional Sobre Estudios Cuantitativos y

Cualitativos de la Ciencia y la Tecnología. La Habana, Cuba. <http://www.sicht.ucv.ve:8080/bvirtual/doc/Documentos%20UCV/10563.htm> Accessed 16.08.09.

Kennedy, D. (1997). *Academic duty.* Cambridge, USA: Harvard University Press.

Kinsella, W. (1997). *Communication and the construction of knowledge in a scientific community: An interpretive study of the Princeton University Plasma Physics Laboratory. (PhD thesis).* New Brunswick, NJ, USA: University of New Jersey.

Kling, R., & McKim, G. (2000). Not just a matter of time: Field difference and the shaping of electronic media in supporting scientific communication. *Journal of the American Society for Information Science, 51*(14), 1306–1320. http://dx.doi.org/10.1002/1097-4571(2000)9999:9999 < : AID-ASI1047 > 3.0.CO;2-T.

Leslie, D. (2002). Resolving the dispute: Teaching is academe's core value. *Journal of Higher Education, 73*(1), 49–73. Available from http://dx.doi.org/10.1353/jhe.2002.0008.

Liu, C. (2010). *Essay on network antecedents in a knowledge production context.* (PhD thesis). Cambridge, MA: Harvard University, Harvard Business School.

López-Carrasco, M. (2013). *Análisis de la producción científico-tecnológica en universidades mexicanas: Comparación Estado de Chihuahúa y otras entidades, 2007-2011. (Master thesis).* Chihuahua, Mexico: Universidad Autónoma de Chihuahua.

López-Ornelas, M., & Cordero-Arroyo, G. (2005). Un intento por definir las características generales de las revistas académicas electrónicas. *Razón y Palabra,* (43), 1–31. <http://www.razonypalabra.org.mx/libros/libros/caracrevelec.pdf> Accessed 16.08.09.

Luna-Morales, M., & Russell-Barnard, J. (2009). *El uso de nuevas tecnologías de información y comunicación científica en el área de partículas elementales: El caso de la física mexicana.* Mexico, D.F., Mexico: Universidad Nacional Autónoma de México. <http://132.248.242.3/~publica/archivos/libros/nuevas_tecnologias_fisica.pdf> Accessed 16.08.09.

Malcher, M., & Lopes, S. (2013). Construyendo una noción de comunicación de la ciencia. *Chasqui,* (122), 74–81. <http://www.revistachasqui.org/index.php/chasqui/article/view/73> Accessed 16.08.09.

Maletta, H. (2009). *Epistemología aplicada: metodología y técnica de la producción científica.* Lima, Peru: Consorcio de Investigación Económica y Social; Centro Peruano de Estudios Sociales; Universidad del Pacífico.

Marca-Altamirano, T. (2011). *Dificultades que tienen los docentes de la extensión Colonche, Ecuador para desarrollar investigación científica en turismo.* <http://www.gestiopolis.com/dificultades-docentes-colonche-ecuador-investigacion-cientifica-turismo> Accessed 16.08.09.

Mariscal-Orozco, J. (2007). Políticas culturales de divulgación de la ciencia: Sesgos y retos. *Apertura,* 7(7), 36–45. <http://www.redalyc.org/articulo.oa?id=68800704> Accessed 16.08.09.

Márquez-Jiménez, A. (2014). Desarrollo académico y producción científica: la sombra del dictaminador. *Perfiles Educativos, 36*(145), 3–10. <http://www.scielo.org.mx/pdf/peredu/v36n145/v36n145a1.pdf> Accessed 16.08.09.

Marsh, H., & Hattie, J. (2002). The relation between research productivity and teaching effectiveness. *Journal of Higher Education, 73*(5), 603–641. Available from http://dx.doi.org/10.1353/jhe.2002.0047.

Martin, K. (2009). *Learning & knowledge production in North Carolina sea turtle conservation communities of practice.* (PhD thesis). Chapel Hill, NC: University of North Carolina.

Martín-Serrano, M. (2006). La vocación de la sociología académica española: Desde el tiempo de las utopías al de la contrautopía. *Revista Española de Sociología,* (6), 106–113. <www.fes-sociologia.com/files/res/6/06.pdf> Accessed 16.08.09.

Mata-Acosta, V. (2008). *Producción y comunicación científica de los investigadores del Instituto de Astronomía de la UNAM. (Master thesis).* Mexico, D.F., Mexico: Universidad Nacional Autónoma de México.

Matzinger-Tchakerian, M. (1996). *Higher education and the creation of knowledge: Scientific research productivity in the OECD higher education system (1985-1994). (PhD thesis)*. Los Angeles, CA: University of California.

Mendoza, S., & Paravic, T. (2006). Origen, clasificación y desafíos de las revistas científicas. *Investigación y Posgrado, 21*(1), 49–75. <http://www.scielo.org.ve/scielo.php?script=sci_arttext&pid=S1316-00872006000100003> Accessed 16.08.09.

Middaugh, M. (2001). *Understanding faculty productivity: Standards and benchmarks for colleges and universities*. San Francisco, CA: Jossey-Bass.

Miguel, S., Gómez, N., & Bongiovani, P. (2012). Acceso abierto real y potencial a la producción científica de un país: El caso argentino. *El Profesional de la Información, 21*(2), 146–153. Available from http://dx.doi.org/10.3145/epi.2012.mar.04.

Morales-Campos, E., & Martínez-Arellano, F. (2011). *Acceso abierto a la producción científica en humanidades y ciencias sociales en la Universidad Nacional Autónoma de México*. In: 77th IFLA World Library Conference, San Juan de Puerto Rico, 13–18 August, 2011. <http://www.ifla.org/past-wlic/2011/104-campos-es.pdf> Accessed 16.08.09.

Moravec, J. (2007). *A new paradigm of knowledge production in Minnesota higher education: A delphi study*. (PhD thesis). Minneapolis, MN: University of Minnesota. <https://www.educationfutures.com/wp-content/uploads/2008/03/dissertation.pdf> Accessed 16.08.09.

Moreno-Castro, C. (2003). La investigación universitaria en periodismo científico. *Ámbitos*, (10), 1–15. <http://www.redalyc.org/articulo.oa?id = 16801006> Accessed 16.08.09.

Mugnaini, R. (2006). *Caminhos para avaliação de adequação da produção científica brasileira: Impacto nacional versus internacional. (PhD thesis)*. São Paulo, Brazil: Universidade de São Paulo. <http://www.teses.usp.br/teses/disponiveis/27/27151/tde-11052007-091052/pt-br.php> Accessed 16.08.09.

Nakkazi, E. (2015). *Lo que los periodistas quieren de los científicos y ¿por qué?* <http://www.scidev.net/america-latina/comunicacion/guia-practica/qu-requieren-los-periodistas-de-los-cient-ficos.html> Accessed 16.08.09.

National Academy of Science (1982). *Scientific communication and national security*. Washington, DC: The National Academies Press. <https://www.nap.edu/catalog/253/scientific-communication-and-national-security> Accessed 16.08.09.

Nieto, M. (1995). Poder y conocimiento científico: Nuevas tendencias en historiografía de la ciencia. *Historia Crítica*, (10), 3–14. <https://dialnet.unirioja.es/servlet/articulo?codigo = 2186922> Accessed 16.08.09.

Núñez-Jover, J. (2006). La ciencia y la tecnología como procesos sociales: Lo que la educación científica no debería olvidar. <http://www.oei.es/historico/salactsi/nunez00.htm> Accessed 16.08.09.

Núñez-Paula, I. (2004). La gestión de la información, el conocimiento, la inteligencia y el aprendizaje organizacional desde una perspectiva socio-psicológica. <http://bvs.sld.cu/revistas/aci/vol12_3_04/aci04304.htm> Accessed 16.08.09.

Olivas-Ávila, J., & Musi-Lechuga, B. (2013). Aprendiendo a usar el Researcher-ID como indicador de la producción científica. *International Journal of Clinical and Health Psychology, 13*, 253–260. Available from http://dx.doi.org/10.1016/S1697-2600(13)70030-9.

Osegueda, M. (2003). *Scientific research productivity and university modernization in Mexico and Argentina*. (PhD thesis). Miami, FL: University of Miami.

Ospina-Rúa, & Toro-Botero, F. (2009). Producción académica del posgrado en aprovechamiento de recursos hidráulicos durante sus primeros 25 años de existencia. *Avances en Recursos Hidráulicos*, (20), 85–96. <http://www.bdigital.unal.edu.co/18508> Accessed 16.08.09.

Pérez-Cázares, M. (2013). La producción del conocimiento. *Enl@ce Revista Venezolana de Información, Tecnología y Conocimiento, 10*(1), 21–30. <http://www.redalyc.org/articulo.oa?id=82326270003> Accessed 16.08.09.

Piedra-Salomón, Y., & Martínez-Rodríguez, A. (2007). Producción científica. *Ciencias de la Información, 38*(3), 33–38. <http://www.redalyc.org/pdf/1814/181414861004.pdf> Accessed 16.08.09.

Piña-Pozas, M. (2007). *Análisis bibliométrico de la revista estudios demográficos y urbanos del colegio de México D.F.* Mexico, D.F., Mexico: El Colegio de México; Biblioteca Daniel Cossío Villegas.

Pires-Noronha, D., & Aguiar-Población, D. (2002). Producción académica de docentes/doctores de los programas de posgrado en ciencia de la información en Brasil. *Revista Ciencias de la Información, 33*(1), 25–33. <http://www2.eca.usp.br/nucleos/pc/artigo/artigo%20cuba2002.pdf> Accessed 16.08.09.

Polanco, X. (2006). Análisis de redes: una introducción. In M. Albornoz, & C. Alfaraz (Eds.), *Redes de conocimiento: Construcción dinámica y gestión* (pp. 79–112). Buenos Aires, Argentina: Red Iberoamericana de Indicadores de Ciencia y Tecnología (RICYT). <http://www.ricyt.org/manuales/doc_view/26-redes-de-conocimiento-construccion-dinamica-y-gestion> Accessed 16.08.09.

Porter, S., & Umbach, P. (2001). Analyzing faculty workload data using multilevel modeling. *Research in Higher Education, 42*(2), 171–196. Available from http://dx.doi.org/10.1023/A:1026573503271.

Prat, A. (1998). Evaluación de la producción científica como instrumento para el desarrollo de la ciencia y la tecnología. *Acimed, 9*(4), 111–114. <http://scielo.sld.cu/pdf/aci/v9s4/aci16100.pdf> Accessed 16.08.09.

Prat, A. (2006). Redes de información científica y tecnológica. In M. Albornoz, & C. Alfaraz (Eds.), *Redes de conocimiento: Construcción dinámica y gestión* (pp. 219–227). Buenos Aires, Argentina: Red Iberoamericana de Indicadores de Ciencia y Tecnología (RICYT). <http://www.ricyt.org/manuales/doc_view/26-redes-de-conocimiento-construccion-dinamica-y-gestion> Accessed 16.08.09.

Prince, M., Felder, R., & Brent, R. (2007). Does faculty research improve undergraduate teaching? An analysis of existing and potential synergies. *Journal of Engineering Education, 96*(4), 283–294. Available from http://dx.doi.org/10.1002/j.2168-9830.2007.tb00939.x.

Raviolo, A., Ramírez, P., López, E., & Aguilar, A. (2010). Concepciones sobre el conocimiento y los modelos científicos: Un estudio preliminar. *Formación Universitaria, 3*(5), 29–36. <http://www.redalyc.org/articulo.oa?id=373534519005> Accessed 16.08.09.

Ríos-Ortega, J. (2006). Evaluación de normalización de las revistas contenidas en el Índice del Consejo Nacional de Ciencia y Tecnología. *Investigación Bibliotecológica, 20*(40), 121–148. <http://www.scielo.org.mx/pdf/ib/v20n40/v20n40a6.pdf> Accessed 16.08.09.

Romanos de Tiratel, S., Contardi, S., & Giunti, G. (2010). Estrategias de difusión del conocimiento en ciencias del hombre: El caso de la Facultad de Filosofía y Letras de la Universidad de Buenos Aires. *Información, Cultura y Sociedad,* (23), 31–62. <http://www.scielo.org.ar/pdf/ics/n23/n23a03.pdf> Accessed 16.08.09.

Rozemblum, C., Unzurrunzaga, C., Banzato, G., & Pucacco, C. (2015). Calidad editorial y calidad científica en los parámetros para inclusión de revistas científicas en bases de datos en Acceso Abierto y comerciales. *Palabra Clave (La Plata), 4*(2), 64–80. <http://www.redalyc.org/articulo.oa?id=350539940001> Accessed 16.08.09.

Saavedra-Fernández, O. (2002). *La producción del conocimiento y las tecnologías de información: Valores, conceptos y herramientas.* La Habana, Cuba: EBSCO Information Services.

Salas-Perea, R. (2000). La calidad en el desarrollo profesional: Avances y desafíos. *Revista Cubana de Educación Media Superior, 114*(2), 136–147. <http://www.bvs.sld.cu/revistas/ems/vol14_2_00/ems03200.pdf> Accessed 16.08.09.

Samar, M., & Ávila, R. (2004). *Guía para la elaboración y publicación de artículos científicos y la recuperación de la información en ciencias de la salud.* Córdoba, Argentina: Universidad Nacional de Córdoba.

Scheunemann de Souza, I. (2006). Redes: Superación de diferencias/potenciación de experiencias. In M. Albornoz, & C. Alfaraz (Eds.), *Redes de conocimiento: Construcción dinámica y gestión* (pp. 215–218). Buenos Aires, Argentina: Red Iberoamericana de Indicadores de Ciencia y Tecnología (RICYT). <http://www.ricyt.org/manuales/doc_view/26-redes-de-conocimiento-construccion-dinamica-y-gestion> Accessed 16.08.09.

Schiavo, E. (2006). La universidad y los conocimientos emergentes en el espacio-tiempo de las TIC. In M. Albornoz, & C. Alfaraz (Eds.), *Redes de conocimiento: Construcción dinámica y gestión* (pp. 163–179). Buenos Aires, Argentina: Red Iberoamericana de Indicadores de Ciencia y Tecnología (RICYT). <http://www.ricyt.org/manuales/doc_view/26-redes-de-conocimiento-construccion-dinamica-y-gestion> Accessed 16.08.09.

Semir, V. (2010). El mutatis mutandis de la comunicación científica en la era del internet. *Artefactos*, *3*(1), 49–79. <http://revistas.usal.es/index.php/artefactos/article/view/8429/8501> Accessed 16.08.09.

Seymour, E., Hunter, A., Laursen, S., & Deantoni, T. (2004). Establishing the benefits of research experiences for undergraduates in the Sciences: First findings from a three-year study. *Science Education*, *88*(4), 493–534. Available from http://dx.doi.org/10.1002/sce.10131.

Sharobeam, M., & Howard, K. (2002). Teaching demands versus research productivity. *Journal of College Science Teaching*, *31*(7), 436–441.

Shults, F. (2005). *An empirical model for assessing academic research levels and capacities of colleges and universities. (PhD thesis)*. Knoxville, TN: University of Tennessee.

Silva, T., & Tomaél, M. (2011). Repositorios institucionales: Directrices para políticas de información. Consideraciones. *Ciencias de la Información*, *42*(3), 39–46. <http://www.redalyc.org/articulo.oa?id=181422295005> Accessed 16.08.09.

Sjøberg, S. (2002). Science and technology education current challenges and possible solutionsIn E. Jenkins (Ed.), *Innovations in science and technology education* (vol. VIII, pp. 201–228). Madrid, España: UNESCO. <http://unesdoc.unesco.org/images/0013/001323/132364e.pdf> Accessed 16.08.09.

Søndergaard, T., Andersen, J., & Hjørland, B. (2003). Documents and the communication of scientific and scholarly information: Revising and updating the UNISIST Model. *Journal of Documentation*, *59*(3), 278–320. Available from http://dx.doi.org/10.1108/00220410310472509.

Sonpal-Valias, N. (1996). *Faculty productivity and career stages: an examination of socialization effects*. (Master thesis). Calgary, Canada: University of Calgary.

Sullivan, T., Mackie, C., Massy, W., & Sinha, E. (Eds.), (2012). *Improving measurement of productivity in higher education* Washington, DC: The National Academies Press.

Tarango, J., Hernández-Gutiérrez, P., & Vázquez-Guzmán, D. (2015). Evaluation of scientific production in Mexican state public universities (2007–2011) using principal component analysis. *El Profesional de la Información*, *24*(5), 567–576. Available from http://dx.doi.org/10.3145/epi.2015.sep.06.

Teixeira-Batista, G. (2006). La publicación científica. *Ambiente & Água*, *2*(2), 3–6. <http://unesdoc.unesco.org/images/0013/001323/132364e.pdf> Accessed 16.08.09.

Thurston, D. (1981). *An analysis of faculty productivity in selected colleges of the Florida State University System*. (PhD thesis). Tallahassee, FL: Florida State University.

Torres-Rodríguez, M. (2013). *Propuestas de promoción de la comunicación científica en docentes e investigadores: caso UACh – Facultad de Filosofía y Letras. (Master thesis)*. Chihuahua, Mexico: Universidad Autónoma de Chihuahua.

Torres-Salinas, D., Bordons, M., Giménez-Toledo, E., Delgado-López-Cózar, E., Jiménez-Contreras, E., & Sanz-Casado, E. (2010). Clasificación integrada de revistas científicas (CIRC): Propuesta de categorización de las revistas de ciencias sociales y humanas. *El Profesional de la Información*, *19*(6), 675–682. Available from http://dx.doi.org/10.3145/epi.2010.nov.15.

Townsend, B., & Rosser, V. (2007). *Initial measures of faculty productivity as evidenced in NSOPF data*. Chicago: American Educational Research Association (AERA).

Treat, T. (2008). *The role of collaboration in knowledge production and technology transfer*. (PhD thesis). Champaign, IL: University of Illinois at Urbana-Champaign.

Trillo-Tinoco, F. (2015). Perfiles científicos: Visibilidad e incremento en la comunicación científica colombiana. *Revista Colombiana de Cardiología, 22*(5), 258–259. Available from http://dx.doi.org/10.1016/j.rccar.2015.07.009.

United Nations Educational, Scientific and Cultural Organization (2000). *Science for the Twenty-First century: A new commitment*. Paris, France: UNESCO. <http://unesdoc.unesco.org/images/0012/001229/122938eo.pdf> Accessed 16.08.09.

United Nations Educational, Scientific and Cultural Organization (2002). *Reunión de especialistas en información científica digital*. Montevideo, Uruguay: UNESCO, Oficina Regional de Ciencia para América Latina y el Caribe.

Universidad Nacional Autónoma de México, Dirección General de Evaluación Institucional. (2016). *Estudio comparativo de universidades públicas mexicanas*. <www.ecum.unam.mx/> Accessed 16.08.09.

Villamón-Herrera, M., Devís-Devís, J., Valencia-Peris, A., & Valenciano-Valcárcel, J. (2007). Características y difusión de las revistas científico técnicas españolas de ciencias de la actividad física y el deporte. *El Profesional de la Información, 16*(6), 605–615. Available from http://dx.doi.org/10.3145/epi.2007.nov.07.

Vogt, C. (2004). *A espiral da cultura científica*. Sao Paulo, Brazil: Folha de Sao Paulo.

Weiss, D. (1998). *The relationship between faculty group development and faculty productivity in higher education. (PhD thesis)*. PA, PA: Temple University.

Westell, M. (2006). Institutional repositories: Proposed indicators of success. *Library Hi Tech, 24*(2), 211–226. Available from http://dx.doi.org/10.1108/07378830610669583.

Zamboni, L. (2001). *Cientistas, jornalistas e a divulgação científica: Subjetividade e heterogeneidade no discurso da divulgação científica*. Campinas, Brazil: Autores Associados.

CHAPTER 3

The New Profile of Information Professionals as Scientific Production and Communication Managers: Identification of Competences

3.1 INTRODUCTION

During the past decades, the scientific and technological advances related to scientific communication, and specifically with publications, have largely influenced the ways in which societies have evolved and even in the ways of establishing interpersonal relationships, including ways of living together, socializing, and working. In the specific case of scientific communication, it is necessary to launch and finance diverse research processes that must result in a series of projects and products. This requires the development of support structures and infrastructures, which must be appropriately defined to ensure that scientific production and communication take place correctly.

All activities related to scientific production and communication become complex procedures, as they imply a series of elements worth considering and that positively contribute to the generation of tangible benefits. Knowledge generation and improvement processes, as well as the incorporation of technologies, methods, and theories are closely related with the human factor. Knowledge generation emerges from such a substantial element, whose ultimate goal is to contribute to innovation and social wellbeing. To disregard the value of teachers and researchers is to deny the rise of new findings.

Scientific and technological development emerges from knowledge institutions (universities and research centers), that are created and developed under the patronage of governmental or private entities. Knowledge institutions become the backbone of knowledge development and the main motivation of the people working in them (researchers, technicians,

The Role of Information Professionals in the Knowledge Economy
DOI: http://dx.doi.org/10.1016/B978-0-12-811222-9.00003-0

professors, managers) lie in research generation as well as in the development of extension and teaching activities (Bailey, 1999; Gómez-Labrada, 2011). Scientific research and communication should not be considered as individual or detached activities. These must be seen as collective and cooperative endeavors, as their development implies the support of several actors that will not necessarily appear in publications' authorship credits. Research results must be made available to society, and their appropriate scientific communication contributes to the generation of new knowledge in the different scientific fields and disciplines.

Given the importance of research and scientific communication as substantial functions of knowledge institutions, several elements have been established to measure them. The development of activities prone to such measurement must be under the direct or indirect responsibility of people who are highly trained to develop certain specific actions that do not necessarily lie within the domain of any professional or researcher. The measurement of research and scientific communication as a specialized activity results in conferring certain metrics and status to researchers and their institutions. It also allows developing appropriate strategies to increase their productivity indexes, both quantitatively and qualitatively, in order to overcome the situation of institutions that only focus on isolated efforts that tend to be low in impact.

Currently, knowledge institutions are used to foster the development of scientific communication processes. However, not every institution possesses significant advances regarding the generation of scientific products, both in quality and quantity. One of the arguments alleged by the actors that can develop research is that they are responsible for too many activities and hence they find it difficult to invest the necessary efforts in order to develop any actions beyond teaching and learning within classrooms. From a global perspective, low scientific productivity can be attributed to: (1) budget limitations; and (2) the lack of epistemological foundations that allow developing appropriate regulations to foster and evaluate scientific communication (González-Nando, 2007; Gorbea-Portal, 2004; Townsend & Rosser, 2007).

Teachers' and researchers' information competences are often reflected in their capacity for transforming research results into scientific communication products (Ramírez-Martínez, Martínez-Ruiz, & Castellanos-Domínguez, 2012; Sancho, 1990). The main difficulty lies in knowing how to conduct the activities required by scientific communication, specifically the systematic and organized development of texts and other communication types; which are only valid if they possess a certain level of quality, that imply the participation of their authors and the support of other actors within the academic environment.

Despite the existence of initiatives to foster scientific production and the availability of government grants to strengthen academic programs, staff, infrastructure and collaboration networks, teachers, and researchers can lack the appropriate models to develop scientific communication products and hence it would not be possible to measure the impact of investments in knowledge institutions (Calvo-Hernando, 2006; Connell, 2004; Lozano-Guadalajara, 1997). In consequence, the generation of scientific communication products represents the fundamental value of knowledge institutions that have appropriately skilled human capital.

It is then a priority to determine strategies to foster knowledge generation through the development of scientific communication products. Such strategies must consider diagnosing the current conditions of teachers and researchers regarding their information competences, because this can either encourage or inhibit knowledge generation (Cortés-Vargas, 2007; Lara-Navarra, 2008). Such a diagnostic allows determining the capacity and adaptability of teachers and researchers as knowledge generators and detecting the elements that were able to emerge from research and that have been projected through scientific communication (Montoya-Contreras, García-Ulloa, & Zamora-Uribe, 2013).

The scientific competences presented in this chapter exceed the recommended competences for teachers and researchers. Hence, they imply the incorporation of an additional actor, who may possess the necessary scientific competences in order to support other research and scientific communication stakeholders. Such an actor is a scientific production and communication manager and this function must be ideally attributed to an information professional. The choice of such a professional as the ideal one to assume this role is grounded in the fact that, among all scientific disciplines, information science is the one that studies diverse information sources, as well as their management, communication, and every other technical, technological, or social process that takes place around information sources. Scientists construct science and transfer it through teaching, but do not necessarily directly contribute toward generating a scientific culture or to the imperative development of scientific competences in their students. In the particular case of information science, its curricula must provide contents related to scientific production, dissemination, and communication, about managing and fostering their emergence, and developing information and scientific competences in others. This makes this discipline's training unique compared to other sciences, considering that information professionals must support the development of other sciences and possess distinct characteristics, such as: problem-solving, constructing representations of diverse kinds of phenomena, and the acknowledgment of the specific functions played by a wide range of diverse scientists.

Information professionals as scientific production and communication managers should contribute to the structuring and creation of scientific productivity environments through the academic support they may offer by conducting diverse specific activities that allow to efficiently convert scientific production into scientific communication.

3.2 SCIENTIFIC COMPETENCES AS KEY ELEMENTS FOR SCIENTIFIC COMMUNICATION

This section is based on the assumption that scientific competences must be present in all the stakeholders involved in scientific production, dissemination, and communication. However, it must be considered that the level of scientific competence that each stakeholder possesses could vary depending on the individual. In the case of information professionals as scientific production and communication intermediaries, their level of scientific competence must be above that possessed by professors or researchers, because they will support scientific processes by taking into account precise methodologies, even if they do not conduct research by themselves.

Scientific competences are understood as the set of knowledge (wisdom), competences (capabilities), and attitudes (willingness) that are manifest in diverse contexts to display the capacity of significantly confronting social challenges involved in producing, appropriating, or applying knowledge in responsible ways (Hernández, 2005; Tobón, 2006; Valdés-Cuervo, Vera-Noriega, & Carlos-Martínez, 2012). From the perspective of scientific thought's potential, scientific competences are not characterized by the mere consultation of documents, but by the situations that mobilize knowledge and the implementation of activities related to its applications, implications, and links to other scientific subjects (Chamizo & Izquierdo, 2007).

Scientific and research competences include cognitive and social processes that are beyond information selection and processing, beyond disciplinary knowledge, these involve a creative and propositional integration of knowledge, the interaction with new situations, problem solving from an ethical perspective and the construction of contextualized meanings (García-Contreras & Ladino-Ospina, 2008). In relation to scientific disciplines, scientific competences adopt two modes: (1) the application of procedures and dexterities to conduct experiments (procedural competences); and (2) data systematization, integration of scientific communication products and achieving their publication, these competences are related to knowledge management (executive competences). While scientists or researchers often center on and have extensive capacity to develop the former mode, information professionals as scientific production and communication managers center on the latter.

In the case of teachers and researchers, their scientific competences refer to their direct and mandatory relationship with their own scientific discipline and with the ability they have for developing systematic, independent, and original research processes. This implies that scientific communication is typical of specialists who are centered on such activity as an essential part of their lives, hence its achievement must not be improvised nor taken lightly.

Information professionals as scientific production and communication managers must have a high level of scientific competence that allows them to be knowledgeable of diverse scientific disciplines. Although it would not be the main purpose, they would be characterized by having an extraordinary capacity, because they would be professionals capable of thinking scientifically and exhibiting a special sensibility and management of the diverse characteristics of scientific communication in the different disciplines.

Regarding scientific communication in knowledge institutions, there are two types of scientific competences: (1) those shown by professors and researchers and that are necessary to develop science and generate knowledge; and (2) those shown by information professionals, which include the applications of tools in order to ensure that scientific production and communication take place, data systematization, integrating reports, structuring contents in scientific documents and developing strategies to ensure that the knowledge created by others is adequately known by other scientific communities or by society in general, through the formal publication of scientific communication or dissemination products.

The development of scientific competences will generate a scientific culture, which includes understanding the social dynamics that are related to science, the ways in which scientific elements are linked, and the interrelations among scientific knowledge producers, which include different interests, practices, codes, norms, and power relationships (Ferrer & León, 2016; Vaccarezza, 2008). The main characteristics of scientific culture are concentrated in the following aspects: (1) it is materialized in the ways in which individuals conduct scientific activities; (2) it emerges from formal training on knowledge-related elements, such as its creation and management; and (3) it includes capabilities related to the analysis, synthesis, and contextualization of the environment in which research is developed (Zamarrón, 2006). Hence, if scientific culture is considered as the acquisition of competences through formal training, this implies that scientifically literate individuals must display a certain scientific sensibility and value scientific knowledge as a fundamental element for the development of society and innovation.

The inclusion of scientific culture in people's everyday life is characterized by the following three criteria: (1) the place of science in culture and globalization is made more prominent; (2) the divide between experts and nonexperts is reduced; and (3) it seeks to develop scientific evaluation and control competences in citizens (López, 2009). In knowledge institutions, scientific culture is delimited by multiple factors and conditions that information professionals must consider in their role of managers:

1. Social organization (organizational structure) and its cultural product (research) may not be supported enough for scientific production and communication to take place (Moya-Anegón et al., 2005;Rodríguez, 2007).
2. The probability of research generation depends on several factors related to researchers, their sociocultural contexts, and the environments in which they act (Simonton, 2009).
3. There are factors that determine professors' behavior regarding their development of knowledge generation processes, such as: institutional demographic characteristics, academic and research track record, human capital, professional status, organizational climate, individuals' motivations, gender, ethnicity, and number of children (Antony & Raveling, 1998; Porter & Umbach, 2001; Toutkoushian & Bellas, 1999).
4. There is a relationship between self-evaluation, self-efficiency, and motivation toward teaching (Russell, 2003) as elements that

knowledge institutions cannot control, but that are decisive for scientific production and communication. Occasionally, there are also differences between female and male professors, because each gender may tend to have greater facility for diverse working roles.

A precise categorization of scientific competences for professors, researchers, and information professionals is based upon the following: (1) willingness toward inquiry (intellectual curiosity); (2) questioning of different interpretations, both their own and those of other people; (3) willingness toward generating knowledge as a daily activity; (4) knowledge of the adequate information sources available and their different quality levels; (5) presentation and representation of ideas in different formats; (6) information selection, ranking, organization, and interpretation; and (7) acknowledging the value of scientific knowledge's social impact and knowledge relationship with society (Hernández, 2005).

It is challenging to identify the concrete processes that allow developing scientific competences in the human resources working at a knowledge institution. Often, professors and researchers acquire scientific competences on a trial-and-error basis or because they have a particular interest that is seemingly innate. The responsibility of developing scientific competences is usually attributed to educational systems, which must foster them through their curricula; but this hardly happens, even if appropriate contents are indeed included, they usually do not have sufficient impact.

The difficulties faced by educational systems in meeting society's current expectations regarding scientific training, globalization, knowledge economy (KE), information and communications technology (ICT), the accelerated growth of knowledge, and the dynamics involved in the evolution of professional profiles, all represent a challenge for adapting to constant change. However, the priority represented by the professional training of an individual in a specific scientific discipline makes educational systems put the development of scientific competences on a secondary level; the training to conduct discipline-related activities is prioritized over the development of competences for communicating science (Álvarez-Lirez, Arias-Correa, Pérez-Rodríguez, & Serralé-Marzoa, 2013).

The training of professors as researchers in scientific production and communication is considered a current issue: although it is difficult to identify the concrete elements that would guarantee the development of scientific competences, it is acknowledged that scientific culture is vital to generate new theories and processes, because current research evaluation criteria do not conceive the figure of a professor who does not conduct research or that lacks a research methodology to investigate their own practice (Coronado-Borja & Arteta-Vargas, 2015; García-Contreras & Ladino-Ospina, 2008). Faced with such a situation, the cited authors propose to initiate scientific training in elementary education, in order to achieve the development of scientific competences from the acquisition of the following elements:

1. Basic competences in relation to the interest and willingness toward research, regardless of the scientific discipline: capacities for presenting and developing written reports, employ a scientific language to communicate ideas related to a project and working in a group.
2. Procedural competences linked with research processes within a specific discipline: capacities for developing experimental processes, implement measuring instruments, consider ethical and security norms, and develop complex thinking.
3. Capacities for working in groups with freedom of expression, participating respectfully and professionally in any discussion about others' opinions, and accepting responsibilities.

Scientific literacy is a means to achieve a scientific culture, however, it is challenging to measure if an individual is scientifically literate (Ferrer & León, 2016; Vaccarezza, 2008). The implementation of scientific literacy can be observed in the design of the Programme for International Student Assessment (PISA), which is applied to 15-year-old students and considers four individual characteristics that determine scientific literacy levels: (1) understanding scientific knowledge; (2) using knowledge to identify elements of the existing knowledge; (3) capacity for acquiring new knowledge (learning to learn); and (4) capacity for explaining scientific phenomena and drawing conclusions based upon evidence (Bybee, McCrae, & Laurie, 2009).

PISA's vision represents a global perspective, although a seemingly indirect one, that allows assessing teenagers' scientific competences for problem solving. The Organization for Economic Co-operation and Development (OECD, 2007) offers another global vision about scientific literacy, defining it as the individual's capacity for understanding the characteristics of science as a form of human knowledge and of research; it also considers science as an element that shapes the intellectual heritage that is related to their specific cultural contexts. According to the OECD, scientific literacy has to do with the willingness that people have toward scientific-related issues and scientific ideas, which generates citizens capable of questioning, reflecting, and constructing new ideas.

These two international perspectives agree in the following aspects that characterize the levels of competence in scientific literacy: (1) the influence of the personal, social, and global aspects that conform individuals' contexts; (2) the scientific knowledge that the individual has acquired in an explicit way (i.e., through their school education), as well as knowledge about scientific processes; and (3) the attitudinal perspective, including the comprehension of the ways in which the individual responds depending on their interests, scientific curiosity, and responsibility. These three aspects determine the scientific literacy that each person can apply in everyday situations. The way in which scientific competences are identified in students (even at an early age), can become contradictory with the conceptualization that professors may have as the people responsible for training subjects with a determined level of competence in scientific literacy.

In a similar way to scientific production and communication processes, the accreditation of scientific competences originates from the need to measure its quality and reach. Hence, every information professional as a scientific production and communication manager must display a high level of competence in scientific literacy, which involves conforming to different assessment, accreditation, and enhancement mechanisms related to the scientific visibility of publications, but the scientific competence of knowledge institutions is also evaluated through the use of rankings developed from the research, production, publication, and innovation data of what their academics produce as a collective (Arévalo, 2014).

It must be considered that university professors and researchers have a double responsibility toward scientific competitiveness. Firstly, because of the need for evidencing their own capacity, and secondly, because of the responsibility they have in developing scientific competences in other subjects. Professors that exclusively work in teaching activities and do not conduct research are practically devoid from the indicators that would allow measuring their scientific competences, because the evidences related to their experiences, profiles, practices, and environments are not considered for this type of measurement, nor are they considered to guarantee the existence of scientific competences in such professors (Martínez-Galaz & González-Weil, 2014).

Regarding graduate students, they are a central group in the study of scientific competences, as it is expected that, because of their educational background, they are subjects with a proven scientific capacity and they should show interest, need, and capacity for research. The manifestation of scientific competences in graduate students can be revealed in different levels: (1) an adaptive capacity to work (knowledge, procedures, and experiences); and (2) personal and human relations qualities, which are evidenced if the subject is capable of appropriating and using scientific methodologies and discourses to create knowledge and communicate it to different groups through scientific publications (ANUIES, 2000; United Nations Educational, Scientific, & Cultural Organization [UNESCO], 2009; Valdés-Cuervo et al., 2012).

3.3 KNOWLEDGE INSTITUTIONS AND SCIENTIFIC COMPETENCES

The responsibility for training human resources capable of conducting research is de facto attributed to knowledge institutions. However, the factors that intervene in such training are not often analyzed in detail and hence such training might not happen in a consistent way. Such factors include stakeholders' personal traits and the elements put in place to foster research (both individual and institutional), which also enable scientific production and communication (Leslie, 2002; Marsh & Hattie, 2002).

The current policies of knowledge institutions propose that scientific research must be projected through the generation of scientific publications and become one of their main activities (Dreze & Debelle, 1983). Knowledge institutions' central commitment has historically varied from the exclusive scheme of professional training into being active in the productive system of knowledge.

Regarding the social function of knowledge production and generation, the positioning of knowledge institutions has had dynamic results, in a personal, collective, organization, and social sense; which includes the comprehension, creative redesign, the concern toward the research applications, and its transformation into scientific communication (Núñez-Paula, 2004). Scientific production and communication are conditioned to diverse organizational aspects, such as: (1) they are uninterrupted processes (developed on a daily basis); (2) they result from the influences that people receive, which are grounded on accumulated experiences (considering the possibility of transferring certain tasks to students as researchers in training); and (3) cultural training patterns that are typical of the organization and of the social values present in its context, i.e., some institutions will assign a higher priority to the training in scientific production and communication than others (Albornoz, 2001; Alves, 1999; Antony & Raveling, 1998).

The training of human resources on knowledge generation and management processes will depend on the institutional availability of the ideal financial, demographic, cultural, and technological conditions; and these vary depending on the institution and even the country (Chauí, 2001; Middaugh, 2001; Saavedra-Fernández, 2002). Hence, the availability of such ideal conditions will have a greater impact on the actual development of scientific production and communication in a knowledge institution than stakeholders' personal interests. Such conditions can be summarized in the following way: (1) contextual factors: organizational climate, resources, and leadership; (2) the relationship between research and public policy; (3) prioritizing research over teaching; (4) procedural factors: the use of data collection instruments to gather feedback; and (5) the existence or lack of indicators that define what is expected from professors and researchers (Canales & Luna, 2003; Díaz-Barriga & Rigo, 2003; Hernández-Castañón, García-Valenzuela, Uicab-Pool, Calini, & Mendes, 2008).

Knowledge institutions are training organizations, as such they enable knowledge retention and accumulation through the gathering of documents resulting from the searches conducted in different sources, but the scientific production and communication managers, as well as professors and researchers, are the people that will work toward obtaining the necessary tools to be able to generate knowledge (Berger & Luckmann, 2001). The integration of scientific findings in published products goes beyond daily activities or personal tastes, they require having adequate training to do so, as well as having the competences for identifying and appropriately using scientific communication channels, correctly applying the elements required by scientific societies, as well as the capacity for structuring scientific documents with the necessary rigor to be accepted and published (UNESCO, 2013).

From a KE perspective, the actual growth of scientific production and communication must transcend the maximization of student enrollment or the quantification of teaching actions as primary activities. Knowledge institutions' new vision brings forth the need to develop actions to train human resources on knowledge management processes to influence the quality of education in general and contribute to a paradigm shift regarding a self-sufficiency in knowledge consumption (Prince, Felder, & Brent, 2007; Sharobeam & Howard, 2002). In a conventional sense, the training of human resources on scientific production and communication indirectly supports teaching within knowledge institutions (Badley, 2002;

Brew, 2003; Elton, 2001; Pocklington & Tupper, 2002). Stimulating research favors a better understanding of studied subjects and fosters the use of quality information sources (Vogt, 2003).

Individuals with a formal education, who have acquired or are perfecting their competences to contribute in scientific production and communication processes, are key stakeholders for generating positive results in knowledge institutions; which will contribute toward the increase of individual and institutional indicators and metrics. Examples of such positive results are: (1) better integration of people to research projects; (2) capacity for selecting and using better information sources; (3) adequate selection of the appropriate scientific channels to communicate research findings; and (4) interest and confidence in accomplishing greater and better scientific publications (Pascarella & Terenzini, 2005). The training experiences for professors and researchers from universities in the US that aim to increase their scientific production and communication levels are characterized by the following areas of opportunity: (1) consulting the needs of professors and researchers; (2) search of scientific information sources; (3) editing and preparation of manuscripts; (4) instruction in the use of data analysis software; (5) diverse workshops; (6) search of academic events for presenting conferences; and (7) diverse services such as access to websites, style manuals, and databases, both commercial and open access (Goodwin, Kozleski, Muth, Rodhes, & White, 2006).

3.4 IDENTIFICATION OF SCIENTIFIC PRODUCTION AND COMMUNICATION COMPETENCES

The needs of professors, researchers, and information professionals as scientific production and communication managers, have allowed to identify diverse practical and specific competences that enable the efficient generation and communication of scientific knowledge. Such competences are grouped into four general categories: information, linguistic, communication, and digital competences (Fig. 3.1); which are intersected and divided in specific and normative criteria that this chapter includes descriptively. These competences result from the combination of diverse perspectives identified in the relevant literature.

It is possible to acquire these four competences through diverse learning actions, both by professor and researcher training and strengthening processes and by the curricula leading to the establishment of professional profiles that focus on developing scientific production and communication

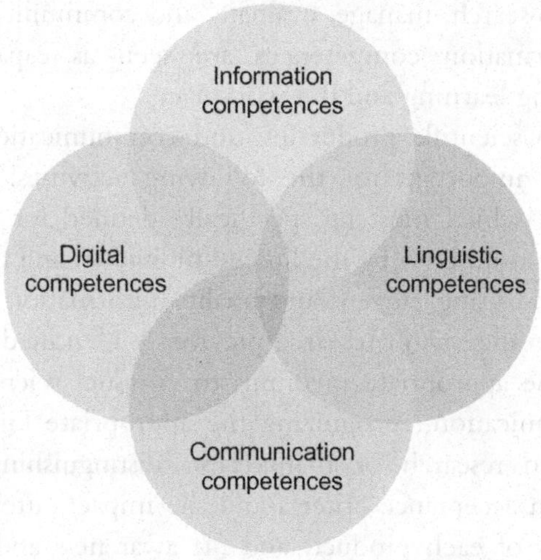

Figure 3.1 Scientific production and communication competences.

managers. For these training processes to happen in a systematic way and for them to have a substantial effect in knowledge institutions, they should be implemented through: (1) the generation of academic support centers, which should be departments specifically dedicated to enable knowledge generation by professors and researchers; and (2) the implementation of structured academic programs of medium reach or in models of continuing education, which must train professors and researchers to continue to increase their scientific production and communication activities independently. Both initiatives demand the engagement of information professionals as scientific production and communication managers.

The research field that identifies the competences that enable scientific production and communication has a close relationship with knowledge management, which is often considered to be within information science. This discipline is mainly focused in quantitative methodologies, but its diversity of works are grounded on positivist, constructivist, or pragmatic paradigms, making use of quantitative, qualitative, or mixed methods, respectively (García-Alsina & Gómez-Vargas, 2015).

3.4.1 Information Competences

From the information science perspective, these are the most studied competences by the information literacy field of research and practice. In general terms, information competences are considered as the group of capacities that enable an individual to know when they need information, as the capacity to search, manage, evaluate, and communicate information adequately. Information competences are seen as capacities that are needed for lifelong learning and the workplace.

In relation to scientific production and communication, information competences are important for the following activities: (1) identifying lines of research, which must be specifically defined for the purpose of knowledge generation, both by the literate individual and their institution; (2) identifying and using current and quality information sources, which must be related to the line of research previously identified; (3) identifying and managing the appropriate mediums to conduct scientific dissemination and communication, recognizing the appropriate kinds of products for a determined research or manuscript, distinguishing their quality levels, publication acceptance criteria and the impact, attention, and visibility possibilities of each product; and (4) awareness and application of the legislations, guidelines, and norms that regulate scientific production and communication regarding ethics and intellectual property rights.

The main characteristics of information competences lie in the capacity for accessing, reading, and interacting with scientific literature. This is considered a central part in the academic role of professors, researchers, and information professionals as scientific production and communication managers (Halevi, Moed, & Bar-Ilan, 2015). The level of information competence is reflected in diverse tasks, such as: the selection of pertinent information and the capacity of distinguishing between scientific dissemination and communication documents, as between primary and secondary sources, and identifying the appropriate and specialized databases for each discipline (Molteni & Chan, 2015).

The development of information competences in higher education has been usually linked to digital or technological competences and they have gained greater relevance in curricula. However, it seems that its impact over scientific production and communication has not been enough. Hence, it is important to appropriately define each specific competence when assuming the holistic perspective of scientific competences.

The importance of information and digital competences is related to: (1) the exponential growth of knowledge production in all disciplines and the own demands of each field; (2) the existence of a larger number of sources dedicated to information storage, organization, and dissemination in various digital formats; (3) the curricular incorporation of diverse pedagogical tendencies that are oriented toward the study of practices and knowledge construction through various didactic activities, which are part of the training of future researchers and scientific production and communication managers who should be capable of searching, selecting, constructing, and communicating knowledge; and (4) the need to train individuals on diverse forms of expression and communication of ideas, opinions, and knowledge in multiple languages and forms of discourse, such as written or spoken, scientific or dissemination discourse, as well as the verbal presentation of contents or using audiovisual media (Area-Moreira, 2010).

3.4.2 Linguistic Competences

Linguistic competences are related to the use of language through the expression and interpretation of concepts, thoughts, feelings, facts, and opinions in order to perform oral and written discussions. Such interactions may take place in diverse social and cultural contexts, which will determine the characteristics of the language written or spoken, such as the grammar, pragmatic, and sociolinguistic characteristics.

Linguistic competences are highly related to communication competences and they are even seen as equal. Within scientific production and communication, linguistic competences are related to the adequate use of language, especially written, and they are characterized by: (1) the adequate use of written language and structuring of content; (2) reading and writing of scientific documents in the reader's native language; and (3) reading, writing, and translation of documents to other non-native languages, particularly in the most used (e.g., English), translation may not indicate a complete proficiency of another language, but it must be good enough to allow its reading and interpretation.

Linguistic competences are also related to information competences, because the correct writing of scientific documents and the description of research findings demand the demonstration of information seeking, selection, compilation, and processing competences, which are supported in the comprehension and production of scientific texts for diverse audiences. Linguistic competences involve a set of skills, knowledge, and attitudes that are interrelated and mutually supported in order to conduct a successful scientific communication that may be destined to different communities or audiences (scientific or the general public), who will be able to understand the communicated knowledge and even use it, provided that they have been correctly materialized from a linguistic point of view.

In any form of training, linguistic competences tend to be wide, transversal, multipurpose, and basic for all individuals, they are also inherent to every scientific culture and discipline (Reyzábal, 2012). These competences are highly related to other individual skills such as reading, because whoever does not read will not be able to write properly. These competences are necessary for the collective interaction and knowledge production of diverse groups of people, either specialists (scientific communities) or the general public (scientific dissemination to all social sectors).

According to international organizations such as the OECD (2007), linguistic competences have diverse applications, especially oral, written, and through the use of ICTs, expressed both in the native language as well as in other languages. However, their application to written language is emphasized, as it is a determining element to publish scientific products that may be registered and measured as part of the scientific communication of an individual, institution, region, or scientific discipline. The use of linguistic competences for the construction of scientific texts and products implies: (1) a certain level of knowledge about the topic that is being developed, which especially comes from the use and management of scientific literature, but without discarding previous knowledge that may have originated from scientific dissemination documents (understood as a cognitive competence); (2) development of individual and collective activities under topical, syntactical, and lexical conventions among the participants; (3) the adequate use of the language goes beyond a correct writing style, it means having the capacity of understanding, deciding, and acting upon criticisms received and distinguish among opinions, facts, hypotheses, theories, laws, and contributions; and (4) capacity of confronting the consequences of what has been expressed in writing, as this is generated knowledge, such ideas become epistemic factors within a scientific discipline that may be either a new contribution or further elaboration from previous ones (Reyzábal, 2012).

The level of application of every competence to scientific production and communication will vary depending on each scientific discipline. Professors and researchers must exhibit a high level of linguistic competences regarding the definition, explanation, argumentation, and justification of the topics they study, at least within their own scientific discipline (Camacho-González & Quintanilla-Gatica, 2008). In contrast, information professionals must acquire several cognitive competences related to the scientific disciplines they collaborate with, but they also should be able to adapt to working with other disciplines. The relationship between linguistic competences and scientific production and communication implies: (1) identifying the contextual elements of what is intended to be communicated; (2) planning scientific production processes; (3) using scientific language adequately and correctly; and (4) applying semantic norms in order to present the texts in a clear and adequate way.

3.4.3 Communication Competences

Communication and linguistic competences are usually combined in the scientific literature. However, when studied from the perspective of scientific production and communication, linguistic competences are more related to knowledge production through an adequate content systematization. In contrast, communication competences have more to do with the application of norms and principles for ensuring that the generated knowledge transcends as a scientific communication phenomenon. This means that they imply seeking the most adequate scenarios for making scientific contents available for scientific communities and society in general, which will vary depending on the kind of content, its depth, and the intentions behind its communication.

Communication competences are considered to be greater than linguistic competences, because they consider sociocultural parameters and include other kinds of languages (mathematical, iconographic, musical, and statistical), which are used transversally; communication competences even give closure to every scientific production and communication process, considering that: (1) their acquisition demands formal and continuous training; (2) they are based in the writing and structuring of scientific contents, as well as the capacity for understanding social customs, cultural habits, and diverse circumstances of each scientific discipline; and (3) they imply the effective use of complex systems of languages, codes, and thoughts (Reyzábal, 2012). Communication competences for the management and communication of scientific knowledge include the comprehension, organization, and construction of scientific texts as a fundamental unit. They also imply the consideration of cognitive, communicational, and sociocultural approaches, the application of a systemic-functional grammar, the study of language and its norms and reveals authors' cognition and their relationship with society (reality).

Communication competences include the set of skills and capacities that enable the appropriate engagement with specific interactional situations, including interpersonal (Aguirre-Raya, 2005). Communication competences have two main manifestations: oral and written. The latter is largely related with scientific communication, because it is vital to publish scientific products with the scientific rigor required by scientific communities.

It is necessary to study communication competences from a multidisciplinary perspective, e.g., psychology acquires a very important role, as it allows analyzing the behavior behind human expression; linguistics allows understanding the configuration of language skills; and pragmatics offer an useful multivariate perspective (Bermúdez & González, 2011).

Researchers keep a direct relationship with and need scientific communication, because it allows them to make public their research findings through specialized publications. The communication competences for scientific production and communication have the following characteristics: (1) they seek to enhance knowledge through scientific communication; (2) before communicating, the researcher must be capable of analyzing data, exhibit a sense of creativity and offer logical statements; (3) from an axiological perspective, these competences must be objective, critical, cultured, ethical, conscious, and demanding; and (4) they are best manifested within constructive and collaborative work, not so much individually (Linares-Herrera & Nápoles-Betancourt, 2012). According to Ghosh and Kshitij (2015), collegiate actions must be regulated and take place thanks to the organization of scientific clusters.

The capacities that conform communication competences and that allow the communication of research findings are: (1) perception and identification of research problems; (2) formulation of scientific problems; (3) accuracy of scientific concepts and signs; (4) distinguishing useful and pertinent information; (5) abstraction capacity for structuring information in a concise way; (6) application of scientific writing style norms; (7) turn scientific results into scientific documents; (8) objective-based group work; and (9) apply ethical guidelines across research and in every scientific product (Esteve-Ramírez, 1999; Lolas-Stepke, 2000). Scientific knowledge generation is aided by different communication media, models, and forms. This means that there is a direct relationship between the development of communication competences, the quality of learning, and the construction of scientific models (Palancino-Rodríguez, 2007).

In essence, communication competences are specifically related to: (1) scientific writing and style correction, an element which relates them with linguistic competences; (2) applying norms for structuring scientific documents under specific formats, using a diversity of style manuals for preparing manuscripts and edited documents; (3) identifying the diverse types of research, because they may influence the structure of manuscripts, both in form and substance; (4) the capacity for developing research protocols and projects; and (5) being capable of enabling relationships and activities with other scientists and scientific communities through the formation of institutional, national, and international networks.

Communication competences are especially relevant when they are integrated together with information competences at the core of information science curricula, because they allow contributing toward: (1) establishing and defining research problems; (2) locating and accessing documents that are pertinent for research; (3) integrating literature reviews through the synthesis of the available documents; (4) designing research; (5) implementing research; (6) managing, processing, and analyzing data; (7) identifying conclusions; and (8) integrating and conducting scientific communication of research findings (García-Marco, 2017). In consequence, communication competences are relevant because they impact all knowledge generation processes.

A vital part of communication competences is that they ensure that scientific language is used correctly for writing the texts to be published (Palancino-Rodríguez, 2007). In order to achieve this, the individual is required to transform natural language into scientific language, thus causing a radical change in the semantics and conceptual conditions in this transition from the former to the latter (Melogno, 2011). Scientific language is aided by style norms, it is characterized by its rigor, and it is aimed at the scientific communities that are constituted by specialists in diverse disciplines (Álvarez, 2001; Domínguez-García, 2009).

3.4.4 Digital Competences

Digital competences, also described as technological competences, are the set of knowledge, skills, attitudes, and behaviors that enable individuals to use ICTs (TIC). These competences allow identifying how technologies work and using them to accomplish specific objectives, solve problems, and make decisions (CRUE-TIC & REBIUN, 2009).

In relation to scientific production and communication, digital competences may be seen under the following perspectives: (1) a fundamental perspective, related to the operation of ICTs; (2) using data-processing software, from the most common such as word processors and spreadsheet managers to statistical analysis software such as Minitab, SPSS, or NVivo (including ATLAS.ti, which is mainly used for managing qualitative data); (3) using software for the editorial design of documents; and (4) conducting successful information search strategies in databases and other digital sources.

Although digital competences are considered to be complementary to the others studied in this chapter, the use of virtual spaces has gained much prominence in higher education during recent decades. Hence, digital competences are vital for facilitating the daily activities of an academic community, as they allow professors, researchers, students, and administrative staff to harness the advantages of models such as e-learning, virtual teaching, hybrid education, blended learning, Massive Open Online Courses (MOOC), Learning Management Systems (LMS), among other digital spaces and alternatives. Implementing ICTs to university teaching requires students and professors to have the necessary competences to handle LMS tools, as well as using the diverse resources of the Web 2.0 (Area-Moreira, 2010).

Digital competences are related to the following areas: (1) software, hardware, and devices; (2) installing and configuring software; and (3) accessing networks and Internet resources, through effective searching and navigation, as well as knowing about network benefits and risks (Repanovici, 2012).

The previous conceptualizations, although valid, are not enough for defining digital competences, as they exclusively center on the measurement of tangible knowledge objects. However, there are also intangible objects that are not usually considered among these competences, but they are important for knowledge society. Such intangible elements that can be considered within digital competences are: (1) technology's raison d'être; (2) the cultural, social, financial, political, and environmental effects of technology; (3) the design of processes, products, and services; (4) the skills needed to research and innovate in new situations; and (5) all professional skills related to technology (Castellanos-Domínguez, Jiménez-Hernández, & Domínguez-Martínez, 2009).

3.5 THE NEW PROFILE OF INFORMATION PROFESSIONALS AS SCIENTIFIC PRODUCTION AND COMMUNICATION MANAGERS

Information science is perhaps one of the disciplines with the largest development of proposals about new professional roles, which have very diverse nuances and application perspectives. Such proposals can be briefly classified in the following way:

1. The construction of new professional profiles for strengthening the discipline from its current curricular conditions (López-Yepes, 2007;

Tejada-Artigas & Martínez-González, 2013). This is probably the most studied aspect and the most prominent perspective is related to the improvement of current curricular contents, by considering successful case studies from different knowledge institutions, which are regularly based upon the saturation of a diversity of contents that, in consequence, is characterized by a wide range of knowledge areas but a low level of specialization.

2. The modernization of the professional exercise, without discarding the work activities performed around the traditional library. For instance, strengthening information services as a support to research activities, which is intended to benefit libraries, knowledge institutions, and researchers (Iribarren-Maestro, Grandal, Alecha, Nieva, & San-Julián, 2015). Another example is related to conducting editorial duties for the journals published by knowledge institutions (Santana & Francelin, 2016). The limitation of this perspective is that the implementation of these new functions are often conceived as taking place exclusively though libraries; seeing this as a limitation is not intended to devalue libraries' importance and participation in scientific endeavors.
3. Analyses of the labor market to determine its requirements, this perspective considers that such a market defines the quality, pertinence, and proficiency of information professionals' profiles for being able to work with information services, capacity development and training, administration and management, information analysis and organization, records management, and ICTs (Gibaja, 2013; Jaramillo, 2015; López-Yepes, 2007). Some experts consider this perspective to be contrary to the purposes of knowledge institutions, as higher education is subordinated to the needs of the labor market, turning education into a sort of commercial academic market.
4. Perspectives grounded in the transition from the industrial society to information and knowledge society and propose opportunity and development areas for information professionals to work in diverse organizations (Alòs-Moner, 2001). These include hybrid professional profiles that are circumscribed to the library sector, but are completely focused on the use of digital mediums and formats for the filtering and selection of contents, as well as for attending specific collectives (Merlo-Vega, Gómez-Hernández, & Hernández-Sánchez, 2011). These futurist visions still imply uncertainties and some proposals have unreal perspectives.
5. Professional exercise in complementary sectors that do not necessarily belong to information professionals' own profile, such as

organizational decision-making computing systems (Muñoz, 2006) or marketing processes (González-Valiente, 2012). It is usually considered that placing any specialist in areas that do not correspond to their field will condemn them to have lower levels of competence than the pertinent specialist; although transdisciplinary actions are positive, a professional should not lose the essence of their own specialty.

6. Information professionals that work according to the new research policies of knowledge institutions and any other institution adopting a smart organization model. Such organizations are characterized by the interaction, innovation, and research capacity (Izquierdo-Alonso, Moreno-Fernández, & Izquierdo-Arroyo, 2008). This perspective is based on developing the profile of information professionals as scientific production and communication managers. It is an answer to the increase and strengthening of research processes in knowledge institutions, the search for processes to increase the efficiency of research groups, train new researchers, and seek newer labor horizons for information professionals within activities that naturally fit their professional profile and objects of study, without invading other professionals' specialties. This perspective implies overcoming the perspective of information professionals' tied working dependence exclusively in libraries, but without necessarily discarding libraries. However, it gives prominence to information professionals within knowledge institutions and it conforms to KE's innovative vision regarding scientific production and communication.

The profile of information professionals as scientific production and communication managers is based upon the following five competences (Fig. 3.2): (1) science evaluation; (2) research processes and types; (3) scientific style and writing manuals; (4) databases and information search strategies; and (5) scientific legislation (Torres-Rodríguez, 2013).

The following sections present a general description of each competence along with their objectives and a selection of the topics they include, which must be studied from the perspective of scientific competences, regarding their demands of knowledge, skills, and attitudes.

3.5.1 Science Evaluation

The objective of this area is to provide a series of theoretical elements and practical tools for conducting information metrics analyses through the application of the practical procedures covered by bibliometrics,

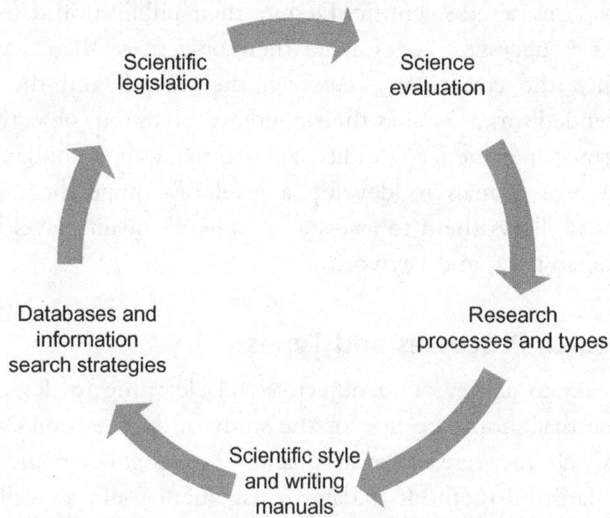

Figure 3.2 Scientific production and communication competences.

infometrics, scientometrics, and altmetrics, as well as any other mechanism for measuring scientific production and communication. These areas allow to measure scientific documents' impact, attention, and the citation networks around them. Science evaluation allows determining the quality of the scientific production and communication of an individual, group, institution, country, or discipline.

The topics included within science evaluation are: conceptual frameworks related to information metrics analyses; publications' flow analysis for accomplishing scientific communication; measurement of scientific literature's growth and age, concentration of scientific literature and measurement of authors' scientific productivity; scientific communication analysis and the establishment of scientific information networks; and the development of strategies for ensuring that researchers and institutions are publishing in such a way that they are ideally indexed in Scopus and Web of Science, and are generating metrics and indicators recognized by bibliometrics, infometrics, scientometrics, and altmetrics; this allows measuring and evaluating the scientific production of researcher institutions according to international standards and developing actions to enhance their competitiveness as knowledge generators.

Due to the excessive abundance of published documents, the use of digital media has great prominence within this area. However, not all documents are relevant enough nor do they all possess the necessary quality to be considered scientific. Despite their publication dates or their timeliness, it is necessary to evaluate their objectives, their writing and syntax quality, the congruence between their depth and the audience they are intended for, as well as their contents' precision, objectivity, coverage, relevance, pertinence, validity, and accuracy. It is fundamental for information professionals to develop a level of competence in science evaluation that allows them to assess a document's quality level by examining its title, abstract, and keywords.

3.5.2 Research Processes and Types

This area seeks to achieve two objectives: (1) learning to determine the research type that should be use for the study of diverse topics and disciplines in which the researcher acts; and (2) recognizing and applying descriptive statistical methods as data-management tools, as well as inferential statistics to draw conclusions, thus aiding the research process and decision-making.

The general topics that allow to cover the needs stated by the mentioned objectives would be: quantitative, qualitative, and mixed-methods research; application of statistical methods for data collection, organization, processing, and presentation; and statistical inference and inferential methods, both parametric and nonparametric. It is pertinent to also include the development of research protocols and projects, the use and handling of statistical data-processing software and the software used for designing figures, tables, and formulas.

3.5.3 Scientific Style and Writing Manuals

The objective of this competence is to familiarize information professionals with the use of the main style manuals for writing manuscripts and those related to the edition of documents, which depend on the scientific discipline. Information professionals must consider the scientific production and communication demands as well as institutional, national, and international standards in order to support researchers.

The application of a certain style manual will depend on the discipline, for example: (1) Social Sciences tend to favor the use of the Publication Manual of the American Psychological Association (APA); (2) Humanities use the Modern Language Association Style Manual and Guide to Scholarly Publishing (MLA); and (3) Natural Sciences and Engineering may use the style of the Institute of Electrical and

Electronics Engineers (IEEE). Many of the cited manuals include editing guidelines, however The Chicago Manual of Style is highly used for structuring, editing, and preparing diverse kinds of documents (articles, books, book chapters, or theses) for their scientific communication. It is also to consider within this competence the use and management of digital journal software, such as Open Journal Systems (OJS); and even platforms for developing open access repositories, such as EPrints or DSpace.

The development of this competence is necessary for correctly preparing scientific documents according to internationally accepted style manuals, which will ensure their quality regarding formal aspects as well as their uniformity, syntax, readability, and correct citation and referencing; hence, this will increase the possibilities for a document to be accepted for publication. The main topics included in this competence are: style schemes for presenting scientific documents; characteristics of each type of scientific document; scientific writing guidelines, citation forms, referencing and writing of abstracts; and basic principles for translating scientific documents.

3.5.4 Databases and Information Search Strategies

The objective of this area is to develop the management and use of scientific information databases and open access resources within research practices. The availability of a wide variety of information resources ensures that researchers will have multiple platforms to choose from in order to conduct advanced and specialized searches; hence, it is important to learn how to distinguish between the academic and scientific resources that may satisfy their needs.

The topics included under this competence are: use of the ICTs used in scientific production and communication; development of information seeking and management processes in the various platforms available; databases and information services, both commercial and open access; identifying scientific communication media depending on their quality levels (dissemination, peer-reviewed, indexed), by considering the use of various indexes such as Web of Science, Scopus, or SCImago, as well as identifying academic events such as congresses or symposia and interest groups or networks.

3.5.5 Scientific Legislation

This is perhaps one of the most worrisome areas, especially because of plagiarism and self-plagiarism situations that may take place in scientific domains. The objective of this area is to familiarize professors, researchers, and scientific production and communication managers with the legal aspects that regulate scientific production and communication. This competence includes diverse topics that will depend upon the participants' environment, such as: international and national laws that govern intellectual property, copyright, and patents; the importance and use of normalized numbers such as ISBN, ISSN, DOI, PubMed, among others; the application and use of copyright alternative schemes such as *Creative Commons*; the diverse conditions that allow researchers to self-archive their manuscripts and publications in open access repositories; and the legal implications of scientific communication evaluation.

The individuals immersed in scientific communication must recognize the elements that protect their creative efforts and how to legally communicate their scientific documents. Although intellectual property laws protect any kind of creation (inventions, literary works, symbols, names, and images), it is a fundamental element in scientific communication. However, scientific legislation is commonly understood as being almost exclusively related to the unlawful use of contents.

REFERENCES

Aguirre-Raya, D. (2005). Reflexiones acerca de la competencia comunicativa profesional. *Revista Cubana de Educacion Medica Superior, 19*(3). <http://scielo.sld.cu/pdf/ems/v19n3/ems04305.pdf> Accessed 16.08.09.

Albornoz, O. (2001). *La reforma de la educación superior y la revolución bolivariana*. Caracas, Venezuela: Universidad Central de Venezuela, Facultad de Ciencias Económicas y Sociales.

Alòs-Moner, A. (2001). El profesional del siglo XXI al servicio de la sociedad y de las organizaciones. *El profesional de la información, 10*(12), 26–29. <http://www.elprofesionaldelainformacion.com/contenidos/2001/diciembre/6.pdf> Accessed 16.08.09.

Álvarez, I. (2001). Problemas en torno a la denominación del lenguaje científico-técnico: Ciencia, técnica, tecnología e ingeniería. *Ibérica: Revista de la Asociación Europea de Lenguas para Fines Específicos*, (3), 31–42. <https://dialnet.unirioja.es/servlet/articulo?codigo=2475901> Accessed 16.08.09.

Álvarez-Lirez, M., Arias-Correa, A., Pérez-Rodríguez, U., & Serralé-Marzoa, J. (2013). La historia de las ciencias en el desarrollo de competencias científicas. *Enseñanza de las Ciencias: Revista de Investigación y Experiencias Didácticas, 31*(1), 213–233. <http://www.raco.cat/index.php/Ensenanza/article/view/285712> Accessed 16.08.09.

Alves, R. (1999). *Professor não vale nada*. Sao Paulo, Brazil: Caderno Especial; Ranking da Ciência; Folha de Sao Paulo.

Antony, J., & Raveling, J. (1998). *A comparative analysis of tenure and faculty productivity: Moving beyond traditional approaches*. Miami, FL: 23rd Annual Meeting of the Association for the Study of Higher Education. <https://eric.ed.gov/?id=ED427598> Accessed 16.08.09.

ANUIES (2000). *La educación superior en el siglo XXI: Líneas estratégicas de desarrollo.* Mexico, D.F., Mexico: Asociación Nacional de Universidades e Instituciones de Educación Superior.

Area-Moreira, M. (2010). ¿Por qué formar en competencias informacionales y digitales en la educación superior? *Revista de Universidad y Sociedad del Conocimiento*, 7(2), 2–5. <http://www.redalyc.org/articulo.oa?id=78016225012> Accessed 16.08.09.

Arévalo, J. (2014). *Alfabetización en comunicación científica: Acreditación, OA, redes sociales, altmetrics, bibliotecarios incrustados y gestión de la identidad digital.* Lima, Peru: Encuentro Nacional de Bibliotecas Universitarias. <http://eprints.rclis.org/22838> Accessed 16.08.09.

Badley, G. (2002). A really useful link between teaching and research. *Teaching in Higher Education*, 7(4), 443–455. Available from http://dx.doi.org/10.1080/13562510276 0553937.

Bailey, J. (1999). Academics' motivation and self-efficacy for teaching and research. *Higher Education Research & Development*, *18*(3), 343–359. Available from http://dx.doi.org/10.1080/0729436990180305.

Berger, P., & Luckmann, T. (2001). *La construcción social de la realidad.* Buenos Aires, Argentina: Amorrortu.

Bermúdez, L., & González, L. (2011). La competencia comunicativa: Elemento clave en las organizaciones. *Quórum Académico*, *8*(1), 95–110. <http://www.redalyc.org/articulo.oa?id=199018964006> Accessed 16.08.09.

Brew, A. (2003). Teaching and research: New relationships and their implications for inquiry-based teaching and learning in higher education. *Higher Education Research & Development*, *22*(1), 3–18. Available from http://dx.doi.org/10.1080/0729436032000056571.

Bybee, R., McCrae, B., & Laurie, R. (2009). PISA 2006: An assessment of scientific literacy. *Journal of Research in Science Teaching*, *46*(8), 865–883. Available from http://dx.doi.org/10.1002/tea.20333.

Calvo-Hernando, M. (2006). *Arte y ciencia de divulgar el conocimiento.* Quito, Ecuador: CIESPAL. <http://www.flacsoandes.edu.ec/libros/digital/43116.pdf> Accessed 16.08.09.

Camacho-González, J., & Quintanilla-Gatica, M. (2008). Resolución de problemas científicos desde la historia de la ciencia: Retos y desafíos para promover competencias cognitivo lingüísticas en la química escolar. *Ciência & Educação*, *14*(2), 197–212. <http://www.redalyc.org/articulo.oa?id=251019505002> Accessed 16.08.09.

Canales, A., & Luna, E. (2003). Cuál política para la docencia? *Revista de la Educación Superior*, *32*(127), 45–52. <http://publicaciones.anuies.mx/pdfs/revista/Revista127_S3A2ES.pdf> Accessed 16.08.09.

Castellanos-Domínguez, O., Jiménez-Hernández, C., & Domínguez-Martínez, K. (2009). Competencias tecnológicas: bases conceptuales para el desarrollo tecnológico en Colombia. *Revista Ingeniería e Investigación*, *29*(1), 133–139. <http://www.scielo.org.co/scielo.php?script=sci_arttext&pid=S0120-56092009000100017> Accessed 16.08.09.

Chamizo, J., & Izquierdo, M. (2007). Evaluación de las competencias de pensamiento científico. *Alambique: Didáctica de las Ciencias Experimentales*, *51*, 9–19.

Chauí, M. (2001). *Escritos sobre a universidade.* São Paulo, Brazil: Universidade Estadual Paulista.

Connell, H. (2004). *University research management: meeting the institutional challenge.* Paris, France: Organisation for Economic Co-operation and Development.

Coronado-Borja, M., & Arteta-Vargas, J. (2015). Competencias científicas que propician docentes de ciencias naturales. *Zona Próxima*, *23*, 131–144. Available from http://dx.doi.org/10.14482/zp.23.5797.

Cortés-Vargas, D. (2007). Medir la producción científica de los investigadores universitarios: La bibliometría y sus límites. *Revista de la Educación Superior*, *36*(142), 43–65. <http://www.redalyc.org/articulo.oa?id=60414203> Accessed 16.08.09.

CRUE-TIC & REBIUN. (2009). *Competencias informáticas e informacionales en los estudios de grado*. Spain: s.n. <http://www.uv.es/websbd/formacio/ci2.pdf> Accessed 16.08.09.

Díaz-Barriga, F., & Rigo, M. (2003). Realidades y paradigmas de la función docente: Implicaciones sobre la evaluación magisterial en educación superior. *Revista de la Educación Superior, 32*(127), 53–61. <http://publicaciones.anuies.mx/pdfs/revista/Revista127_S3A3ES.pdf> Accessed 16.08.09.

Domínguez-García, I. (2009). Un acercamiento al lenguaje del texto científico. *VARONA*, (48-49), 67–72. <http://www.redalyc.org/pdf/3606/360636904010.pdf> Accessed 16.08.09.

Dreze, J., & Debelle, J. (1983). *Concepções de universidade*. Fortaleza, Brazil: Edições UFC.

Elton, L. (2001). Research and teaching: Conditions for a positive link. *Teaching in Higher Education, 6*(1), 43–56. Available from http://dx.doi.org/10.1080/13562510020029590.

Esteve-Ramírez, F. (1999). *Comunicación especializada*. Madrid, Spain: Editorial Tucumán.

Ferrer, A., & León, G. (2016). Cultura científica y comunicación de la ciencia. *Razón y Palabra*, (65). <http://www.razonypalabra.org.mx/N/n65/actual/aferrer_gleon.html> Accessed 16.08.09.

García-Alsina, M., & Gómez-Vargas, M. (2015). Prácticas de gestión del conocimiento en los grupos de investigación: Estudio de un caso. *Revista Interamericana de Bibliotecología, 38*(1), 13–25. <http://www.scielo.org.co/pdf/rib/v38n1/v38n1a1.pdf> Accessed 16.08.09.

García-Contreras, G., & Ladino-Ospina, Y. (2008). Desarrollo de competencias científicas a través de una estrategia de enseñanza y aprendizaje por investigación. *Studiositas, 3*(3) 7–16. <https://dialnet.unirioja.es/servlet/articulo?codigo=3717381> Accessed 16.08.09.

García-Marco, F. (2017). The relevance of communicative competence in the context of information literacy programs. In D. Sales, & M. Pinto (Eds.), *Pathways into information literacy and communities of practice: Teaching approaches and case studies* (pp. 135–164). Oxford, UK: Chandos Publishing. Available from http://dx.doi.org/10.1016/B978-0-08-100673-3.00006-X.

Ghosh, J., & Kshitij, A. (2015). Examining the emergence of large-scale structures in collaboration networks: Methods in sociological analysis. *Sociological Methods & Research*, 1–43. Available from http://dx.doi.org/10.1177/0049124115606153.

Gibaja, V. (2013). El bibliotecario como profesional de la información: Horizontes laborales más allá de la biblioteca. *Información, Cultura y Sociedad, 29*, 49–76. <http://eprints.rclis.org/23458> Accessed 16.08.09.

Gómez-Labrada, A. (2011). Dinámica investigativa en relación con la dimensión docente y extensionista. *Didasc@lia: Didáctica y Educación, 2*, 89–102. <https://dialnet.unirioja.es/servlet/articulo?codigo=4228272> Accessed 16.08.09.

González-Nando, E. (2007). *La investigación científica en la Universidad Nacional Autónoma de México: Un perfil bibliométrico*. (PhD thesis). Spain: Universidad de Murcia. <https://digitum.um.es/xmlui/handle/10201/153> Accessed 16.08.09.

González-Valiente, C. (2012). *El profesional de la información como gestor de mercadotecnia: Aproximación a un importante rol*. La Habana, Cuba: Editorial Universitaria. <http://eprints.rclis.org/23686> Accessed 16.08.09.

Goodwin, L., Kozleski, E., Muth, R., Rhodes, L., & White, K. (2006). Establishing a center to support faculty research. *Innovative Higher Education, 30*(4), 251–268. Available from http://dx.doi.org/10.1007/s10755-005-8347-z.

Gorbea-Portal, S. (2004). *Producción y comunicación científica latinoamericana en ciencias bibliotecológicas y de la información. (PhD Thesis)*. Madrid, Spain: Universidad Carlos III de Madrid.

Halevi, G., Moed, H., & Bar-Ilan, J. (2015). Accessing, reading and interacting with scientific literature as a factor of academic role. *Publishing Research Quarterly, 31*(2), 102–121. Available from http://dx.doi.org/10.1007/s12109-015-9404-9.

Hernández, C. (2005). ¿Qué son las competencias científicas? *In Foro Educativo Nacional: Competencias científicas* (pp. 32–52). Colombia: Ministerio de Educación Nacional. <http://www.colombiaaprende.edu.co/html/mediateca/1607/articles-128237_archivo.pdf> Accessed 16.08.09.

Hernández-Castañón, M., García-Valenzuela, M., Uicab-Pool, G., Calini, M., & Mendes, I. (2008). Barreras y estrategias para la divulgación de conocimiento de enfermería en México. *Desarrollo Científico de Enfermería, 16*(10), 429–433. <http://www.index-f.com/dce/16/r16-429.php> Accessed 16.08.09.

Iribarren-Maestro, I., Grandal, T., Alecha, M., Nieva, A., & San-Julián, T. (2015). Apoyando la investigación: nuevos roles en el servicio de bibliotecas de la Universidad de Navarra. *El Profesional de la Información, 24*(2), 131–137. <http://www.elprofesionaldelainformacion.com/contenidos/2015/mar/06.html> Accessed 16.08.09.

Izquierdo-Alonso, M., Moreno-Fernández, L., & Izquierdo-Arroyo, J. (2008). Grupos de investigación en contextos organizacionales académicos. Una reflexión sobre los procesos de cambio y los retos futuros. *Investigación Bibliotecológica, 22*(44), 103–141. <http://www.scielo.org.mx/scielo.php?script=sci_arttext&pid=S0187-358X2008000100007> Accessed 16.08.09.

Jaramillo, O. (2015). Pertinencia del perfil de los profesionales de la información con las demandas del mercado laboral. *Revista Interamericana de Bibliotecología, 38*(2), 111–120. Available from http://dx.doi.org/10.17533/udea.rib.v38n2a03.

Lara-Navarra, P. (2008). *Estudio de la producción científica en Cataluña: Metodología de análisis y resultados de 15 años de ciencia catalana.* (PhD thesis). Barcelona, Spain: Universidad Pompeu Fabra.

Leslie, D. (2002). Resolving the dispute: Teaching is academe's core value. *Journal of Higher Education, 73*(1), 49–73. Available from http://dx.doi.org/10.1353/jhe.2002.0008.

Linares-Herrera, M., & Nápoles-Betancourt, A. (2012). El investigador científico, un comunicador loable: La interrelación médica-investigativa. *Bibliotecas: Anales de Investigación, 8*(9), 210–215. <http://eprints.rclis.org/25299> Accessed 16.08.09.

Lolas-Stepke, F. (2000). Ética de la publicación médica: Legalidad y legitimidad. *Acta Bioethica, 6*(2), 283–291. <http://www.redalyc.org/articulo.oa?id=55460207> Accessed 16.08.09.

López, A. (2009). El concepto de cultura científica en la sociedad global. *Politeia, 32*(42), 31–55. <http://www.redalyc.org/articulo.oa?id=170014942002> Accessed 16.08.09.

López-Yepes, J. (2007). El nuevo profesional de la información, del conocimiento y de la comunicación: El bibliotecario universitario. *Anales de Documentación,* (10), 263–279. <http://eprints.rclis.org/12097> Accessed 16.08.09.

Lozano-Guadalajara, J. (1997). *Análisis bibliométrico de la producción científica en la revista "Rehabilitación" (1967-1995).* (PhD thesis). Murcia, Spain: Universidad de Murcia.

Marsh, H., & Hattie, J. (2002). The relation between research productivity and teaching effectiveness. *Journal of Higher Education, 73*(5), 603–641. Available from http://dx.doi.org/10.1353/jhe.2002.0047.

Martínez-Galaz, C., & González-Weil, C. (2014). Concepciones del profesorado universitario acerca de la ciencia y su aprendizaje y cómo abordan la promoción de competencias científicas en la formación de futuros profesores de Biología. *Enseñanza de las Ciencias, 32*(1), 51–81. Available from http://dx.doi.org/10.5565/rev/ensciencias.852.

Melogno, P. (2011). Lenguaje científico, traducibilidad y esquemas conceptuales. *Enl@ce: Revista Venezolana de Información, Tecnología y Conocimiento, 8*(2), 11–25. <https://dialnet.unirioja.es/servlet/articulo?codigo=3703543> Accessed 16.08.09.

Merlo-Vega, J., Gómez-Hernández, J., & Hernández-Sánchez, H. (2011). *Estudio FESABID sobre los profesionales de la información: Prospectiva de una profesión en constante evolución.* Madrid, Spain: Fundación Germán Sánchez Ruipérez; Swets. <http://eprints.rclis.org/18057> Accessed 16.08.09.

Middaugh, M. (2001). *Understanding faculty productivity: Standards and benchmarks for colleges and universities*. San Francisco, CA: Jossey-Bass.

Molteni, V., & Chan, E. (2015). Student confidence/overconfidence in the research process. *The Journal of Academic Librarianship, 41*(1), 2–8. Available from http://dx.doi.org/10.1016/j.acalib.2014.11.012.

Montoya-Contreras, J., García-Ulloa, H., & Zamora-Uribe, J. (2013). La divulgación de la ciencia como condición de posibilidad para la generación de conocimiento y la invención científica. *Revista Iberoamericana para la Investigación y el Desarrollo Educativo*, 10. <http://cenid.org.mx/memorias/cdic/index.php/CDIC/article/view/45> Accessed 16.08.09.

Moya-Anegón, F., Chinchilla-Rodríguez, Z., Corera-Álvarez, E., Vargas-Quesada, B., Muñoz-Fernández, F., & Herrero-Solana, V. (2005). Análisis de dominio institucional: la producción científica de la Universidad de Granada (1990-1999). *Revista Española de Documentación Científica, 28*(2), 170–195. <http://redc.revistas.csic.es/index.php/redc/article/viewFile/167/221> Accessed 16.08.09.

Muñoz, B. (2006). El profesional de la información digital: Aspectos organizativos. *Anales de Documentación*, (9), 143–163. <http://revistas.um.es/analesdoc/article/view/1331/1381> Accessed 16.08.09.

Núñez-Paula, I. (2004). La gestión de la información, el conocimiento, la inteligencia y el aprendizaje organizacional desde una perspectiva socio-psicológica. <http://bvs.sld.cu/revistas/aci/vol12_3_04/aci04304.htm> Accessed 16.08.09.

Organisation for Economic Co-operation and Development (2007). *Higher education and regions: Globally competitive, locally engaged*. Paris, France: Organisation for Economic Co-operation and Development.

Palancino-Rodríguez, F. (2007). Competencias comunicativas, aprendizaje y enseñanza de las ciencias naturales: Un enfoque lúdico. *Revista Electrónica de Enseñanza de las Ciencias, 6*(2), 275–298. <http://reec.uvigo.es/volumenes/volumen6/ART4_Vol6_N2.pdf> Accessed 16.08.09.

Pascarella, E., & Terenzini, P. (2005). *How college affects students: A third decade of research* (Vol. 2San Francisco, CA: Jossey-Bass.

Pocklington, T., & Tupper, A. (2002). *No place to learn: Why universities aren't working*. Vancouver, Canada: University of British Columbia.

Porter, S., & Umbach, P. (2001). Analyzing faculty workload data using multilevel modeling. *Research in Higher Education, 42*(2), 171–196. Available from http://dx.doi.org/10.1023/A:1026573503271.

Prince, M., Felder, R., & Brent,, R. (2007). Does faculty research improve undergraduate teaching? An analysis of existing and potential synergies. *Journal of Engineering Education, 96*(4), 283–294. Available from http://dx.doi.org/10.1002/j.2168-9830.2007.tb00939.x.

Ramírez-Martínez, D., Martínez-Ruiz, L., & Castellanos-Domínguez, O. (2012). *Divulgación y difusión del conocimiento: las revistas científicas*. Bogotá, Colombia: Universidad Nacional de Colombia. <http://www.bdigital.unal.edu.co/8394> Accessed 16.08.09.

Repanovici, A. (2012). Professional profile of digital repository manager. *Library Hi Tech News, 29*(10), 13–20. Available from http://dx.doi.org/10.1108/07419051211294473.

Reyzábal, M. (2012). Las competencias comunicativas y lingüísticas, clave para la calidad educativa. *Revista Iberoamericana sobre Calidad, Eficacia y Cambio en Educación, 10*(4), 64–77. <http://www.redalyc.org/articulo.oa?id=55124841006> Accessed 16.08.09.

Rodríguez, J. (2007). *La sociología académica*. Barcelona, Spain: Universidad de Barcelona.

Russell, J. (2003). *Los indicadores de producción científica por género: Un caso especial*. Madrid, Spain: Tercer Taller de Obtención de Indicadores Bibliométricos.

Saavedra-Fernández, O. (2002). *La producción del conocimiento y las tecnologías de información: Valores, conceptos y herramientas*. La Habana, Cuba: EBSCO Information Services.

Sancho, R. (1990). Indicadores bibliométricos utilizados en la evaluación de la ciencia y la tecnología: Revisión bibliográfica. *Revista Española de Documentación Científica, 13*(3–4), 842–865.

Santana, S., & Francelin, M. (2016). O bibliotecário e a editoração de periódicos científicos. *Revista Brasileira de Biblioteconomia e Documentação, 12*(1), 1–25. <https://rbbd.febab.org.br/rbbd/article/view/543/483> Accessed 16.08.09.

Sharobeam, M., & Howard, K. (2002). Teaching demands versus research productivity. *Journal of College Science Teaching, 31*(7), 436–441.

Simonton, D. (2009). Varieties of (scientific) creativity a hierarchical model of domain-specific disposition, development, and achievement. *Perspectives on Psychological Science, 4*(5), 441–452. Available from http://dx.doi.org/10.1111/j.1745-6924.2009.01152.x.

Tejada-Artigas, C., & Martínez-González, B. (2013). *Perfiles profesionales del Sistema Bibliotecario Español: Fichas de caracterización*. Madrid, Spain: Consejo de Cooperación Bibliotecaria. <http://travesia.mcu.es/portalnb/jspui/bitstream/10421/6841/1/perfilesprofesionalesSBE.pdf> Accessed 16.08.09.

Tobón, S. (2006). *Aspectos básicos de la formación basada en competencias*. Talca, Chile: Mesesup.

Torres-Rodríguez, M. (2013). *Propuestas de promoción de la comunicación científica en docentes e investigadores: Caso UACH—Facultad de Filosofía y Letras.* (Master thesis). Chihuahua, Mexico: Universidad Autónoma de Chihuahua.

Toutkoushian, R., & Bellas, M. (1999). Faculty time allocation and research productivity: Gender, race, and family effects. *The Review of Higher Education, 22*(4), 367–390. Available from http://dx.doi.org/10.1353/rhe.1999.0014.

Townsend, B., & Rosser, V. (2007). *Initial measures of faculty productivity as evidenced in NSOPF data.* Chicago: American Educational Research Association (AERA), 2006.

United Nations Educational, Scientific and Cultural Organization (2009). *Conferencia Mundial sobre la Educación Superior, 2009: La nueva dinámica de la educación superior y la investigación para el cambio social y el desarrollo.* Paris, France: United Nations Educational, Scientific and Cultural Organization.

United Nations Educational, Scientific and Cultural Organization (2013). *El decenio de las Naciones Unidas para la educación con miras en desarrollo sostenible (enero 2005- diciembre 2014).* Paris, France: United Nations Educational, Scientific and Cultural Organization. <http://unesdoc.unesco.org/images/0015/001540/154093s.pdf> Accessed 16.08.09.

Vaccarezza, L. (2008). *Exploraciones en torno al concepto de cultura científica* (p. 110). Madrid, Spain: FECYT: Resúmenes del Congreso Iberoamericano de Ciudadanía y Políticas Públicas de Ciencia y Tecnología.

Valdés-Cuervo, A., Vera-Noriega, J., & Carlos-Martínez, E. (2012). Competencias científicas en estudiantes de posgrado de ciencias naturales e ingenierías. *Sinéctica: Revista Electrónica en Educación*, (39), 1–16. <http://www.scielo.org.mx/pdf/sine/n39/n39a12.pdf> Accessed 16.08.09.

Vogt, C. (2003). *Espiral da cultura científica.* Sao Paulo, Brazil: Folha de Sao Paulo.

Zamarrón, G. (2006). De cultura científica y anexas. In A. Marín, C. Pacho, I. Trelles, & G. Zamarrón (Eds.), *Universidad, comunicación y ciencia: Contrastes* (pp. 129–145). Mexico, D.F, Mexico: Universidad Autónoma de Baja California; Porrúa.

CHAPTER 4

An Academic Model to Support Scientific Production and Communication

4.1 INTRODUCTION

There are currently several proposals that allow identifying better levels of scientific literacy competence among citizens (United Nations Educational, Scientific, & Cultural Organization, 2005). There are also initiatives that are carried out by knowledge institutions in order to establish formal education and scientific culture programs. Although knowledge institutions resort to a basic literacy that is only based on the use of information resources, current institutional requirements demand the development of scientific and digital literacies, which result in the generation of an institutional scientific culture, characterized by the presence of environments that are favorable for scientific productivity to take place.

Information literacy must include scientific and digital literacies training and this will be most effective if it is included in the various curricula and if professors implement related actions. Hence, scientific culture is part of education's general purpose. However, there are contradictions in the ways training processes take place, because scientific and digital literacies are considered among the key objectives of education (Fundación Telefónica, 2014), but at the same time traditional educational processes are still being provided (more behaviorist than constructivist) and as such they are extraneous to the possibility of generating an adequate scientific literacy in students and meaningful learning (Villaruel-Fuentes, 2012).

This chapter is centered in a support model to aid knowledge institutions in developing best practices in scientific production and communication. The implementation of this model requires the presence of scientific literacy initiatives and certain levels of competence in the community, because its members must exhibit behaviors that are typical of a strong scientific education, which could have been developed formally or informally throughout their educational background, it may be embedded

The Role of Information Professionals in the Knowledge Economy
DOI: http://dx.doi.org/10.1016/B978-0-12-811222-9.00004-2

in individuals' personal traits as a scientific vocation, or through teaching or professional work experiences.

Regardless of the origin of professors' and researchers' scientific training, they must possess a high level of competence in scientific literacy and hence they must have a scientific culture. However, this does not necessarily occur within all knowledge institutions, because the individual and collective (institutional) measurement of scientific communication competitiveness has become a common assessment parameter for everyone involved in teaching and research processes as a career.

Nowadays, the measurement of scientific communication competitiveness in knowledge institutions requires them to produce research and scientific communication. The scientific development of a knowledge institution can occur under two perspectives that are not mutually exclusive: (1) when research processes emerge from members' efforts, merits, and willingness toward a scientific spirit and despite working under adverse conditions; and (2) when scientific communication emerges from the development of educational and scientific policies which make research a mandatory, shared, and desirable process by a country's education system (Giraldo, Abad, & Díaz, 2005). For some knowledge institutions that have maintained teaching as their exclusive activity, the latter perspective has made them suddenly realize that their consonance with educational-scientific policies and their competitiveness compared to other institutions is limited, by not prioritizing research together with teaching, their scientific production has been scarce or nonexistent and hence they do not have the necessary indicators to meet the criteria of any scientific production evaluation. Other more balanced institutions, which prioritize the development of both teaching and research, have found another reason to reinforce such vision; one that does not imply neglecting educational processes, but that requires giving more importance to knowledge generation.

The transition of teaching as the exclusive activity of knowledge institutions toward scientific production and communication has meant a radical change in the functions of traditional professors, which has originated a particular evolution in the activities of such institutions. In some cases, this transition has meant a disorganized transformation, but incorporating research activities has allowed those teaching-oriented institutions to develop direct and necessary connections with technology, innovation, industry, and society, because knowledge generation from research is an essential function of knowledge institutions (Bedoya, 2003; Rojas-Betancur, 2011).

The mechanisms to foster professors' and researchers' scientific production and communication can be improved by: (1) the changes experienced by institutional productivity environments, which are key for nurturing a scientific culture; (2) the willingness of every individual involved, which also includes their competences and previous experiences; and (3) the application of systematic mechanisms based upon trial and error to scientific activities (Goodwin, Kozleski, Muth, Rhodes, & White, 2006). The strength of an individual's scientific culture will vary depending on their own conditions and experiences. Hence, knowledge institutions must actively establish and develop their own institutional cooperation models in order to enhance scientific activities. Such models must consider the importance of embedding the participation of information professionals as scientific production and communication managers, or even advisors (see Chapter 3: The New Profile of Information Professionals as Scientific Production and Communication Managers: Identification of Competences).

4.2 OBJECTIVES AND SCOPE OF THE PROPOSED MODEL

The scientific production and communication support (SPCS) model that is proposed in this chapter can be considered for: (1) establishing an academic support department with a formal organizational structure within any knowledge institution; (2) a service offered by the staff of a given department within the institution, such as the library or other academic departments; or (3) an independent service that maintains a direct and independent relationship with every professor and researcher requesting it. Despite having an institutional reach, the mentioned options seek to establish individual relationships, but at the same time they should generate relationships with other scientific communities, researchers (within the institution and from other institutions), publishers, scientific journals, and knowledge institutions from every possible context and anywhere in the world. The objectives of the SPCS model are the following:

1. Analyze professors and researchers needs in relation to the development of specific processes to start or continue their scientific production activities, with the perspective of formally and systematically enabling scientific communication through diverse products (scientific articles, books, book chapters, patents, norms, and technical reports).
2. Generate academic support services through mechanisms that aim to push, sustain, and aid research groups with the identification of the

information sources that are pertinent to lines of research within different scientific disciplines (Martín-Sampere & Rey-Rocha, 2007).

3. Participate in the integration of solid and adequate research programs, so that scientific communication is related to the institution's mission and vision.
4. Contribute to the identification of the suitable and appropriate media for scientific communication, that according to current demands, must be peer-reviewed and indexed. The SPCS model must ensure that the quality of the products generated can meet the requirements of such media and as such they can be published.
5. Actively participate in adjusting manuscripts according to requirements of language, writing, intellectual property (avoiding plagiarism and self-plagiarism), the correct use of style manuals, and follow-up on the results from each peer review, which may be of acceptance, adjustment, or rejection.
6. Register the institution's scientific communication longitudinally, both for individual researchers and for the various collectives (research centers or groups and at an institutional level), by taking into account the different types of products and developing information metrics studies (citation studies, impact factor levels. and categorizing publications according to their quality). This allows defining and monitoring the growth and competitiveness levels of the institution regarding scientific production and communication.
7. Systematically assess professors' and researchers' satisfaction with SPCS's initiatives and services by using quantitative and qualitative methodologies to collect and develop proposals for its continuous improvement and finding new ways of individual collective support.
8. Offer continuing education programs on scientific production and communication, adapting them to professors' and researchers' needs according to their different profiles: those already benefiting from SPCS's services, new staff, and those with little or no previous experience on the subject.

This list of objectives is not exhaustive, but these are considered to be the main objectives of the SPCS model and they can obviously be extended depending on the knowledge institution's own needs and conditions, as well as its availability of human resources and infrastructure. Knowledge institutions with adequate scientific productivity and culture levels will tend to seek greater challenges after they accomplish these basic objectives, such as analyzing the institutional competitiveness and comparing it to local, national, and international contexts.

4.3 ORGANIZATIONAL STRUCTURES PROPOSED

It is complex to identify organizational structures without resorting to the basic principles that govern companies, especially when trying to adapt their models to knowledge institutions, which are organizations that may be considered atypical, because they must specialize in professional training, creativity, innovation, and knowledge generation at the same time. When a professor or researcher is tasked with creating ideas, conducting research processes, and communicating findings in scientific documents, they are being granted with a condition of total freedom. Such a situation does not necessarily mean ceasing to circumscribe such professor's or researcher's actions to a functional and bureaucratic scheme, as academic activities cannot take place under purely anarchic models.

Scientific communication represents the crowning point of a set of complex processes, which are usually formal and represent the ways in which knowledge institutions work. Hence, three organizational structures are proposed as alternatives for implementing the SPCS model: (1) formal and independent structures, through the generation of new departments that are integrated to the institution, with their own staff and infrastructure, and directly subordinated to the institutions' highest hierarchy levels; (2) formal structures that depend on an existing department and that work using that department's available resources. Given the nature of scientific production and communication, this structure is usually related to research departments, libraries, or even with scientific laboratories; and (3) informal structures that may originate from the formal structure of the institution and consist of dynamic work relationships among the members of the community (namely professors, researchers, and scientific production and communication managers; as the first two belong to the formal structure).

The first two structures can be more feasible in any knowledge institution, as they are based on already available resources. The first structure allows legitimizing the creation of a department or service that is formally designed to develop scientific production and communication functions; while the second structure allows to reassert the pertinence of the department that will assume the development of the SPCS model. The third option represents the occurrence of complex and dynamic processes whose results are difficult to schedule and predict, as it is a less tangible structure within the institution and hence it can act unnoticed.

Each structure proposed has its own strengths and weaknesses. However, the purpose of this chapter is not to drive the choice over which might be the most convenient, as this will depend on each knowledge institution's own circumstances. It is important for these kinds of structures to emerge from a systematic research process as its empirical basis, this way they can be adapted to the particular needs of an institution. Other aspects that need to be considered when configuring these structures are scientific policies as well as the disciplines and lines of research of the country where the institution is located as well as the scientific disciplines the institution specializes in.

Regardless of the chosen structure, its operation as a structure must be formal and systematic, so the SPCS model can be implemented and achieve its objectives. The next sections detail five coordination mechanisms that are versatile enough to be implemented in any kind of knowledge institution that wishes to apply the SPCS model: mutual collaboration, direct supervision, standardization of working processes, standardization of working products, and standardization of competences and knowledge (Barone, 2009; Hintze, 2006; Mintzberg, 1983; Montana & Charnov, 1993). The description of these mechanisms has been made general enough so that they can be applied to different contexts. These mechanisms emerge from the idea that the structure of an organization is defined by the sum of its processes and the work they conduct is divided into different tasks that are appropriately coordinated to achieve the stated objectives. These five mechanisms are not mutually exclusive, a knowledge institution may decide which to use and in which combination, as they complement each other and none excludes the advantages of the other.

4.3.1 Mutual Collaboration

This way of working is effective if the objectives are accomplished through the mutual collaboration of the institutions' members with the same level. Collaboration is largely informal, although there may be formal manifestation, but it has a generally disjointed behavior. Collaboration among members works from trust and the struggles for achieving specific objectives that may be unrelated to the organization's purposes. However, when participants behave with integrity regarding their commitments, these good intentions are recognized among the collaborating members and they define the results that must be achieved in their own terms. An example of this kind of structure is seen in the use of social media for accomplishing a common endeavor.

Using mutual collaboration with the purpose of generating a structure that will implement the SPCS model usually happens in knowledge institutions without the maturity required for generating the appropriate environments for scientific productivity to take place. In such a situation, informal and formal work relationships can generate scientific production and communication based upon personal and disciplinary affinity; without necessarily implying that the quality or quantity of results will be registered. The actions undertaken by professors and researchers emerge spontaneously, voluntarily, and might be related (or not) to their knowledge institution's scientific policy; which can be solid and well-established, inadequate in its conception, socialization, and dissemination, or inexistent. Unless an information professional proactively supports professors and researchers within mutual collaboration and they recognize the value of this information professional, the institution will not see the need or reason to employ such professionals.

Fig. 4.1, which shows the mutual collaboration mechanism and a working approach that is similar to a coordination mechanism, represents the incipient emergence of scientific production and communication processes. It also indicates the opportunity of incorporating an academic support department or service to fulfill SPCS's objectives and to define

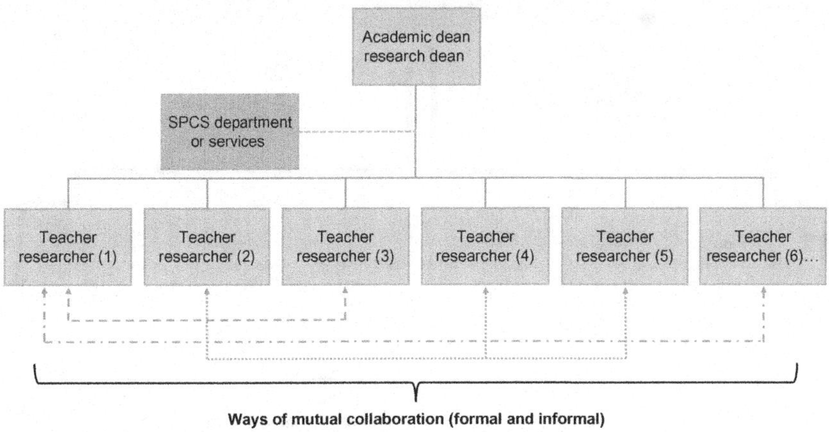

Figure 4.1 Mutual collaboration mechanism.

scientific work policies. Among the groups of professors there may be some experienced members as well as novices, and many of them will not be involved in scientific production and communication; either because of a lack of interest or insufficient training.

4.3.2 Direct Supervision

Direct supervision is manifested when a higher hierarchical authority assumes the responsibility over others' work, issuing instructions and monitoring activities. Direct supervision has the following characteristics: (1) its fundamental aim is to ensure that work is conducted in an orderly, coordinated, and formal manner; and (2) it seeks to enable the best possible productivity environments by improving collaborators' motivation.

This second coordination mechanism, represented in Fig. 4.2, consists of a more rigid bureaucratic structure. However, there is greater interest in formalizing scientific production and communication processes, it promotes a better defined scientific policy and focuses on formal and informal collaboration mechanisms among the members of the academic community. This mechanism is usually managed by an academic or research department and it may be seen as an evolution of the mutual collaboration mechanism.

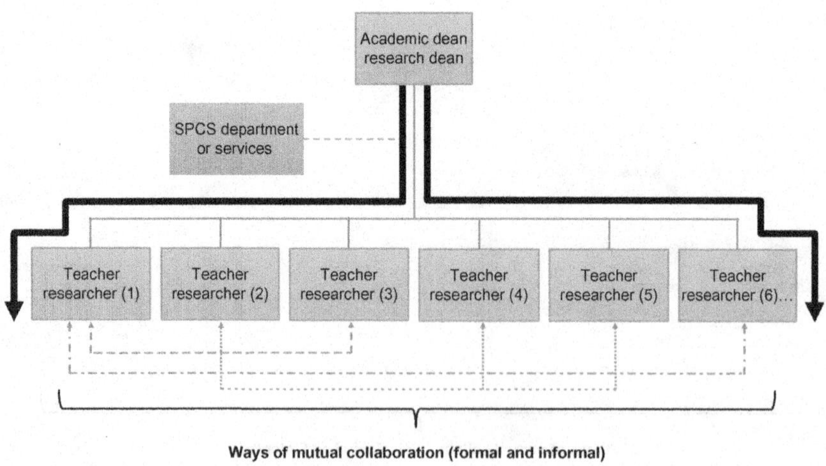

Figure 4.2 Direct supervision mechanism.

4.3.3 Standardization of Working Processes

This third coordination mechanism consists of activities that are formally established or programmed for developing products that are related to the measurement of the individual behavior of an organization's members. This does not imply excluding the presence of formal or informal collaborative work. Some of the distinctive characteristics of the standardization of the working process mechanism are: (1) it seeks to establish a stable behavior regarding the generation of products and services of homogeneous quality; and (2) it strives to generate consistent results and so it also standardizes and legitimizes work conditions.

Fig. 4.3 represents the standardization of processes as a means of identifying uniform ways of working for each member of the academic community. For instance, this mechanism seeks to define new individual ways of working by studying individuals' behaviors and measuring all academic and scientific production. This mechanism proposes the organizational dependence of the SPCS service to a particular department, such as libraries or laboratories; which will count with the presence of the scientific production and communication manager.

4.3.4 Standardization of Working Products

The fourth coordination mechanism refers to the organizations that focus on the characteristics and conditions of the generated products, which

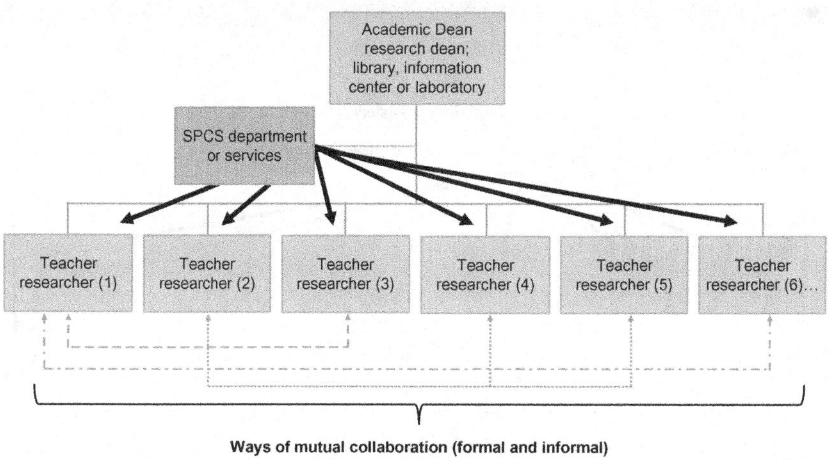

Figure 4.3 Standardization of working processes.

will arguably make this the most adequate option for generating tangible goods. This option seeks to develop products that are destined for specific sectors, hence, the generated products will cater to the needs of a specific market.

Regarding scientific communication, the standardization of the working products mechanism is the ideal organizational mechanism for measuring results. Under this approach, knowledge institutions need to generate specific policies that must establish the minimum scientific products that must be developed individually and collectively, by taking into consideration professors' and researchers' interests and international standards' quality specifications regarding scientific communication.

Scientific articles are usually the most valued scientific communication products, especially those published in scientific journals with an impact factor. However, other quality elements should be considered, such as citations or any other metric or altmetric index. The quality and quantity of products must be defined and standardized in the institutional scientific policies. Moreover, these policies should consider the guidelines specified by the national and international organisms that evaluate and define the scientific competitiveness levels of individuals, groups, and organizations. This structure, represented in Fig. 4.4, also defines the quality measurement of the products that are exclusively generated through formal working relationships.

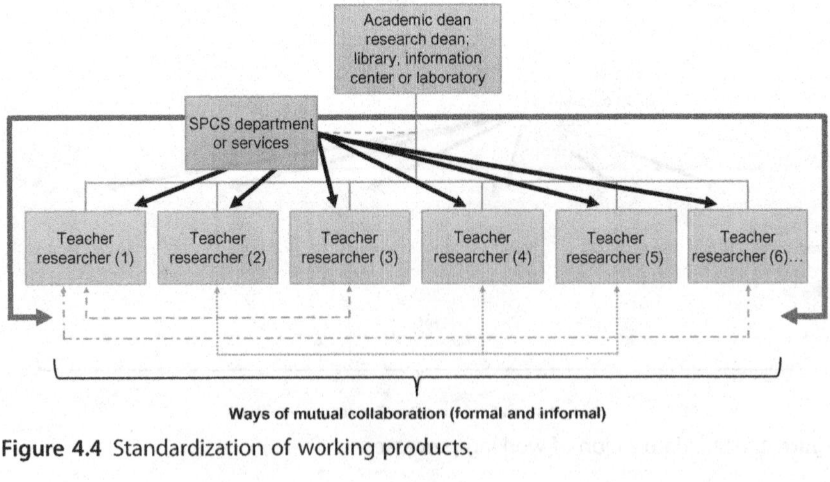

Figure 4.4 Standardization of working products.

4.3.5 Standardization of Competences and Knowledge

The fifth coordination mechanism occurs when work is enabled by the specialized training that each member of the institution has and that allows them to perform adequately; such training is based upon knowledge and competences. This mechanism does not represent a strict organizational structure, but it seeks to standardize research groups by their specialty instead of by their work or results. Each individual uses mutual collaboration and there is little direct supervision, as everyone knows exactly which processes and products they will develop.

According to Fig. 4.5, the standardization of competences and knowledge mechanism represents the most adequate way of working of a knowledge institution that aims to be characterized by the quality of its scientific production and communication. The basis of this vision lies in specialized knowledge, which is regularly acquired through academic degrees, research experience, and academic awards. This mechanism has a direct relationship with the knowledge economy and it consists of the precise measuring of a knowledge institution's scientific competitiveness, by evaluating its scientific communication and prioritizing the individuals that are trained and enabled to generate knowledge.

The standardization of competences and knowledge mechanism allows research groups and lines of research to implement scientific communication strategies. Such strategies are the means to conduct formal

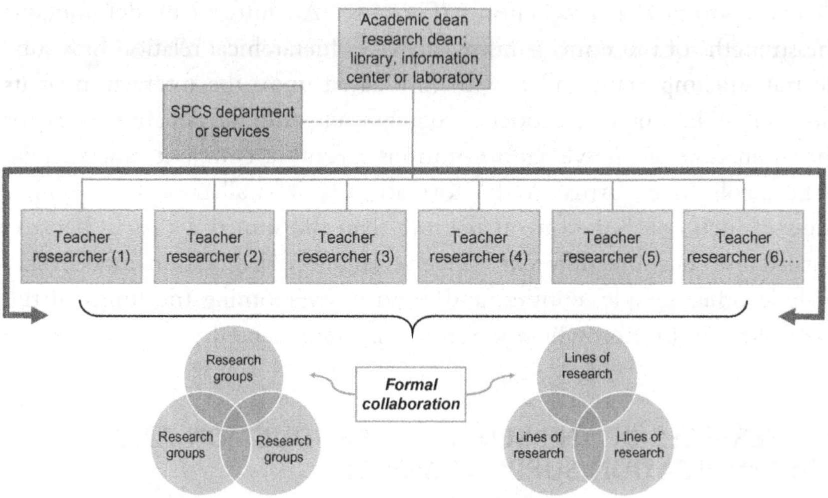

Figure 4.5 Standardization of competences and knowledge.

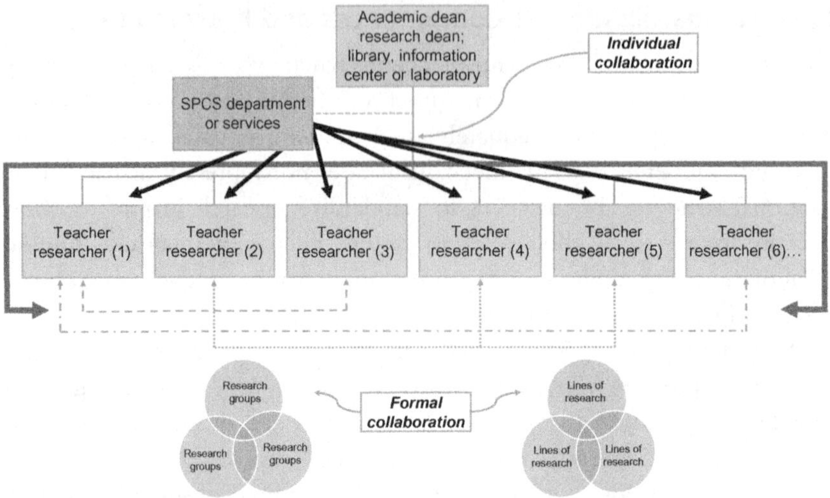

Figure 4.6 Integral model for an SPCS department or service.

collaboration, although informal collaboration might also take place. Research groups and lines of research must be precisely defined to ensure that the generation, recording, and measurement of scientific products correspond to institutional, national, and international guidelines.

4.3.6 Development of an Integral Model

An integral model for an SPCS department or service consists of merging all five coordination mechanisms (Fig. 4.6). An integral model contains the strengths of those mechanisms, it makes hierarchical relationships subtle but still important and it is mainly based upon the interaction of its elements. This integral model recognizes all kinds of collaborations for the evaluation of knowledge institutions' scientific competitiveness (individual, collective, formal, and informal) as well as all possible combinations of such collaborations. It is more than the sum of its parts, because it takes into account different cooperation and collaboration models that include other people, entities, and regions, overcoming the limits of the knowledge institution where the model is implemented.

4.4 SERVICES OF THE SCIENTIFIC PRODUCTION AND COMMUNICATION SUPPORT MODEL

Every knowledge institution has its own environment, which determines the diverse conditions that affect the operation of the SPCS model. The main aspects in which the environment can affect its functional structure are: (1) the allocation of a physical and structural space where its actions will take place, which could be defined within an autonomous department, a restricted service that depends on another department or an independent service that is coordinated by a higher hierarchy in the institution; (2) staffing, from a scientific production and communication manager who will provide the SPCS services, as well as sufficient staff to cater to the various institutional needs, such as translators, statisticians, technicians, and linguists; and (3) the allocation of other resources, e.g., informational (physical and digital) and technological (software and hardware).

Although the context will be decisive for the structure of an SPCS model, the scientific productivity conditions that characterize the knowledge institution where it will be applied can also largely affect such a structure. The development of the SPCS model should consider its evaluation, which will allow determination of the necessary adjustments that need to be done to the model in order to offer better services as scientific culture evolves and it is strengthened by professors' and researchers' work and experiences with the SPCS. Other factors that influence the SPCS are the scientific culture of all involved, their interests and motivations, as well as the institution's support for the development of the SPCS.

Considering that knowledge institutions' contexts are always different, the following sections provide a series of the basic services that the SPCS department can provide: (1) information needs diagnostics; (2) searching for information sources; (3) identification of information sources for scientific communication and dissemination; (4) editing and preparing manuscripts for publication; (5) data transcription, preparation, processing, and analysis; (6) translation of scientific documents; (7) information metrics studies; (8) user satisfaction analysis; and (9) integrating and developing training programs. Table 4.1 presents an approximation to the scientific production and communication competences that are required to develop and provide each of the SPCS services; such competences are classified in linguistic, communication, digital, and information (see Chapter 3: The New Profile of Information Professionals as Scientific Production and Communication Managers: Identification of Competences).

4.4.1 Information Needs Diagnostics

The purpose of developing information needs diagnostics is to clearly and precisely identify the demands for services that can contribute concrete

Table 4.1 Comparison between services and competences

Services of the scientific production and communication support model	Scientific production and communication competences			
	Linguistic	**Communication**	**Digital**	**Information**
Information needs diagnostics		✓		✓
Searching for information sources			✓	✓
Identification of information sources for scientific communication and dissemination			✓	✓
Editing and preparing manuscripts for publication	✓	✓	✓	
Data transcription, preparation, processing, and analysis			✓	
Translation of scientific documents	✓	✓		
Information metrics studies			✓	✓
User satisfaction analysis	✓	✓	✓	✓
Integrating and developing training programs	✓	✓	✓	✓

solutions to answer professors' and researchers' needs regarding scientific production and communication. It allows offering pertinent solutions if diagnostics are conducted at several moments: (1) at the beginning, when the SPCS model is implemented and its user base has been established; (2) when the SPCS is functioning and, in the short term, any time users demand immediate solutions through direct inquiries; and (3) at the medium to long term, when the services have evolved because of higher demand of its users.

Early diagnostics results are useful to determine the structural and functional characteristics that the SPCS should have. The model implemented by each institution will not necessarily include all the services described below, just those that are useful to cover their needs. The methodological implications to develop a diagnostic can vary, the simplest ways can consist of interviewing professors and researchers in brief individual meetings, telephone calls, or by using digital platforms such as email or social media (Goodwin et al., 2006). The diagnostic can also be conducted in a more complex way by implementing research processes, which must be mainly qualitative and participatory, as they allow identifying the needs and improvement opportunities that can be useful to research groups, lines of research, and to the scientific disciplines present in the institution (Torres-Rodríguez, 2013). In all cases, it is recommended to list the needs in order of priority.

Diagnosing needs allow to determine multiple variables that will depend upon the institution's contexts and can also be combined with other kinds of studies, such as systems analysis, studies of specific information needs, users' satisfaction studies, and organizational auditing processes (Goñi-Camejo, 2008). Diagnostic measurement must include professors' and researchers' particular needs and also different contextual aspects, such as: institution type, organizational structure, the scientific products that are currently developed, staff suitability, Information and communications technologies (ICT) availability and conditions for their use, and scientific information resources. It is also fundamental to determine professors' and researchers' academic training, their level of competence regarding scientific literacy, their scientific culture, research experience, scientific communication evidences (that allow evaluating their quality and quantity), and any other aspect that can be useful to design objective work plans (Grover, 1993; Pérez-Morfi, Núñez-Paula, Font-Graupera, & Lazcano-Herrera, 2013).

Due to the fact that the SPCS must work with real and potential users, it is necessary to clearly establish the areas of interest, demand, or need when performing a diagnostic regarding scientific production and communication, as they are closely related to the development of an institutional scientific productivity environment (Fernández-Valdés & Núñez-Paula, 2007). Collected data allow the preparation of users' profiles, which should contain: disciplines of interest, main activities (research, academic, scientific), their knowledge about and their level of use regarding information sources and language proficiency (Hernández-Salazar, 2013).

Information needs diagnostics are objective studies and their results must address concrete situations and aid decision-making. Collected data must allow determining strategies to address particular institutional needs, and their satisfaction should enable better and higher scientific production and communication (Gendina, 2017).

4.4.2 Searching for Information Sources

Every research is based upon an initial review of the pertinent and current scientific literature, which represents a state of the art of the situation under study. Searching for information sources is perhaps one of the SPCS functions that generates the most expectations and allows scientific production and communication managers to know about the scale of professors' and researchers' work during various stages of search, initial or consecutive.

Given that professors and researchers are already familiar with certain specific information sources, the people responsible for the SPCS service should exceed users' expectations, by taking into consideration that they should facilitate a wide variety of scientific sources with a certain level of quality regardless of the format (physical or digital) and identifying their genres, types, reach, and purpose (Martínez, 2013). The basis of adequate information retrieval lies in defining search strategies from users' needs, considering that they will have high-quality standards that may be far from what could be easily retrieved in the Web or found during daily activities, although there are exceptions.

The aspects under consideration to accurately identify the information sources that will be useful to support scientific production and communication processes are: (1) analyze correctly the topic under study, understand its meaning, focus, and reach; (2) identify the keywords most commonly used to represent the topic, using disciplinary thesauri if necessary, and consider different keyword combinations to conduct advanced searches; and (3) characterize the sources retrieved (Martínez, 2013; MSPS, 2009).

In order to offer this service, the scientific production and communication manager should ensure that the institution's available information resources are used optimally. Given the changes and advances regarding scientific information formats (which are mostly acquired in digital before print), the use of specialized databases with access to the main scientific journals is considered vital to satisfy professors' and researchers' needs, because they allow tracking the current findings in the topics of interest.

4.4.3 Identification of Information Sources for Scientific Communication and Dissemination

Searching for information sources is useful for providing research with a theoretical basis and also to communicate research results. The SPCS model must consider both purposes and give preference to the use of peer-reviewed and indexed sources, because if they are used for research, they ensure that the scientific communication products derived from research will have the necessary quality to be published in such kinds of sources.

One of the recommended SPCS activities is the development of peer-reviewed and indexed publications directories by disciplines or lines of research, in order to provide professors and researchers with concrete alternatives for publishing their products. In any discipline, access to the lists of journal titles of the highest level and their metrics is restricted to indexes such as Web of Science, Scopus, and Scimago Journal & Country Rank; the first two are available through commercial subscriptions, while the latter is freely available although it is powered by Scopus data. Data contained in these indexes (and also in others of lesser importance or popularity) allow to develop the mentioned directories of publications by disciplines or lines of research and according to the needs that the SPCS must satisfy. In order to develop more comprehensive directories, it is necessary to consider data from various indexes. Web of Science tends to be the most valued index and in general is given preponderance over others because it is the one that calculates the impact factor, the most well-known metric regarding scientific journals' quality; however, impact factor is also among the most criticized metrics.

Scientific journals are the main tools for scientific communication and, in consequence, scientific articles are the optimal means to make research findings known, especially considering the following: (1) they offer scientific results in the short term; (2) they are the kinds of documents considered by most information metrics studies; and (3) they are most commonly used to communicate research findings for the first time and those considered as primary sources (Betancourt-López, 2003). Given the importance of scientific journals, any SPCS service should consider the characteristics and requirements from those of the highest quality (Ramírez-Martínez, Martínez-Ruiz, & Castellanos-Domínguez, 2012). However, other scientific communication channels with different purposes should not be dismissed, such as books, book chapters, patents, and conferences; because they allow to increase the number of channels through which research findings are communicated and, hence, they allow increasing research visibility.

4.4.4 Editing and Preparing Manuscripts for Publication

This service consists of providing advice regarding scientific writing and adapting manuscripts to the different style manuals used by publications. This includes revisions of the formal elements of a manuscript as well as its contents, which requires high levels of competence regarding scientific writing, manuscript editing using various style manuals, and knowledge about different citation and referencing styles.

Scientific writing goes beyond a simple style of writing using the grammar rules from the language used, it also involves other particular and essential characteristics, such as: precision, clarity, brevity, and formality. Scientific writing demands deep knowledge and experience in the topic that is being communicated. This should be taken into consideration by the SPCS, because the person who will review manuscripts will be a person other than the authors.

Regularly, professors and researchers find scientific writing less difficult given their previous experiences writing manuscripts. However, they find it challenging to adapt a manuscript to a different style manual than the one they are already accustomed to. Sometimes, there is even some resistance toward using different styles, although they are established guidelines for presenting manuscripts. While scientific writing is related to the use of grammar and linguistics, style manuals represent the guidelines that typify, harmonize, standardize, homogenize, and make uniform the criteria used for presenting manuscripts worthy of publication.

Manuscript editing using style manuals represents the application of structural norms. However, the situation is complicated to a certain extent for two reasons: firstly, because there are various manuals, such as the Publication Manual of the American Psychological Association (APA), The Chicago Manual of Style, or the Modern Language Association Style Manual and Guide to Scholarly Publishing (MLA), among others; and secondly, because every journal might request the application of additional adaptations, considerations, or conditions over those stated by a given manual, or they could even require to combine criteria from different styles.

Scientific writing is vital for knowledge communication and it reflects a manuscript's quality, because its language and presentation could delay or prevent its publication, moreover, scientific journal editors or peer reviewers do not tend to edit or modify articles' writing, they just recommend that it should be done appropriately (Griffies, Perrie, & Hull, 2013). Although the scientific format used for manuscripts may seem confusing and rigid for some less experienced professors and researchers, it is the best medium to communicate research results in an efficient, orderly, and logical way; and it also makes it possible to selectively read some of its component parts depending on the reader's needs, e.g., reading just the title, abstract, methodology, results, analysis, tables and graphs, conclusions, or references, without necessarily having to review the entire document (Bates College, 2011). It can be concluded that the content is the form and the form is the content, because they are equally important for assessing the quality of manuscripts.

4.4.5 Data Transcription, Preparation, Processing, and Analysis

Conducting research demands investing a large amount of time in data transcription, preparation, processing, and analysis, which are key activities that make research findings trustworthy and sound. Hence, an SPCS service can offer a support function for using data analysis software (e.g., SPSS or Minitab for quantitative research and NVivo for qualitative research) and it can even provide fundamental statistical advice. Given the characteristics of this service, it can also involve providing training in different modalities and educational spaces.

4.4.6 Translation of Scientific Documents

English is commonly considered scientific communication's lingua franca, this situation makes translation an important SPCS service for those knowledge institutions located in countries where the official language is not English. However, English-speaking institutions could also consider this service for translation to other languages in order to increase accessibility and hence the visibility of the research they produce. These kinds of translations used to be called scientific, technical-scientific, or technical translations, such expressions are occasionally used interchangeably, but when the technical denomination is used, it is usually more related to the translation of industrial documents, while the scientific term is mostly used for the translation of documents produced in knowledge institutions. In non-English-speaking countries, translation represents the possibility of vastly increasing the visibility of generated contents. Other aspects that make English translation important are: (1) communicating findings in a universal language; (2) it allows avoiding authors' cultural bias in their contents; and, (3) it makes it possible to compete with authors from other countries (Franco-Aixelá, 2013).

Given the level of specialization required by a translation service, it requires a very specific profile from the translator, which has the following characteristics: (1) they should be dedicated exclusively to this activity; (2) they must be familiarized with the topics related to the research they translate, in order to use technical terms adequately; (3) they should obtain supplementary skills related to the culture of the country where manuscripts might be published and the usual expressions of the language they are translating into; and (4) general writing competences and high capacity for lifelong learning.

Scientific translation is a highly difficulty service, as it demands a high level of specialization and brings forth situations such as: (1) difficulty in understanding the original text because of a limited understanding of the topics; (2) finding grammar and contextual difficulties; and (3) the translated text might be substantially different from the original because the translator would have needed training or a deeper understanding of the research field they were translating (Freyre, 1999). Generally, specialized translation and specifically that from fields such as natural sciences or medicine, are required to be performed by professionals with high levels of translational (translation techniques and procedures), linguistic-cultural, textual, and documentary competences, as well as conceptual knowledge of the scientific discipline they are translating (Corpas-Pastor, 2001; Martínez-López, 2009).

Under any circumstance, this SPCS service is a great challenge for those countries that pretend to use any language other than the official for scientific communication. It is relevant to point out that it is hardly appropriate to demand an information professional that is working as a scientific production and communication manager to have translation competences, because such a competence is not part of their usual profile; hence, the SPCS must have staff specialized in translations.

4.4.7 Information Metrics Studies

Measuring scientific communication quality and competitiveness in knowledge institutions corresponds to information professionals with practical knowledge and experiences with bibliometrics, infometrics, scientometrics, and altmetrics. Its main purpose is to quantify the behavior of scientific communication during specific periods of time, both in terms of quantity and quality.

Information metrics are seldom considered in some countries and such kinds of studies are not carried out systematically or permanently in many knowledge institutions. These kinds of studies should not be conducted to merely comply with the requirements from an institutional evaluation performed by outside parties, nor should they be done only once, they are usually done with the aim of determining and monitoring individual and institutional conditions regarding scientific production and communication (Chiroque-Solano, 2016).

The improvement of scientific production and communication in knowledge institutions must be based upon scientific methods and aiming for institutional growth, by comparing the behaviors registered in different periods of time through the analysis and evaluation of scientific activities. Metric studies are an important SPCS service as long as they: (1) provide sound and trustworthy indicators to identify the conditions of the scientific communication they measure; (2) their results allow assessing and comparing individual, institutional, geographic, and disciplinary conditions; (3) they support the redefinition of research groups and lines of research through the detection of institutional strengths, weaknesses, and quality levels; and (4) their results contribute to the identification, definition, and redefinition of scientific policies.

Currently, the scientific competitiveness of knowledge institutions is being measured through indicators that are directly and indirectly linked to scientific communication quality, hence, metric studies provide knowledge management processes with a different perspective (Gorbea-Portal, 2013). Moreover, the interesting part of such a kind of measurement is that it allows analyzing data in a transdisciplinary manner and uses results in diverse contexts related to organizational operation and continuous improvement.

4.4.8 User Satisfaction Analysis

The main focus of any organization is related to the characteristics, demands, and conditions of its clients, who determine the consumption of services and goods and largely sustain their operation. In the case of knowledge institutions, specifically related to SPCS models, their clients have very particular conditions given their culture, academic background, and the nature of their demands for specialized services. In the case of the SPCS, its clients are professors and researchers immersed in scientific activities and which it is best to identify as users.

These users can be defined through Martín-Moreno's (2007) vision of information users that need support to develop their scientific activities and all their demands will originate from such activities. For SPCS services, it is important to distinguish between potential and real users, because they are both important for ensuring knowledge institutions' performance.

Measuring user satisfaction can be carried out in three basic ways: (1) measuring potential dissatisfaction, which consists of assessing users' conditions through the praise they manifest toward other similar services; (2) analyzing availability and readiness, which consists of measuring whether the resources and services have been available and ready when they are needed, as well as counting those demands that were satisfied and those that were not; and (3) measuring perceived quality, by collecting users' perceptions toward the service (Hernández-Salazar, 2011; Rey-Marín, 2000).

4.4.9 Integrating and Developing Training Programs

Training has the purpose of enabling users' independence and self-sufficiency in scientific production and communication processes and one of the aims of the SPCS services must be to achieve a state where the majority of the community will not depend upon them in the long term to conduct their scientific activities. This independent-user development process can be understood as the establishment or accomplishment of a satisfactory scientific culture, which can be achieved through two training alternatives: (1) formal, through comprehensive programs with a base of systematically structured contents, which can range from a certification program to a full academic degree related to scientific training, its results will have a medium- to long-term impact; and (2) continuing education, integrated by isolated courses and workshops about specific topics that aim to solve concrete training issues or deficiencies, its results will have a short-term impact. Any training program must address areas of opportunity identified while diagnosing needs (Maya-Ampudia, Ángeles-Zavala, & Camarena-Olmedo, 2014).

SPCS users are adults immersed in the workplace and with self-sufficient academic training, so it is necessary to use an andragogy perspective to the development of training contents, instruction delivery methods, and the evaluation of SPCS training programs. This is usually achieved by adopting the theoretical vision of learning communities or communities of practice, as well as respecting and acknowledging individual learning styles. The challenges of such programs are large, because they raise high and precise expectations from the users regarding receiving innovative training with clear practical applications.

Andragogy centered in learning demands the presence of several critical elements, which makes it different from traditional pedagogic models, such as: (1) planned training programs are goal-oriented, so they must be clearly defined; (2) the professor is seen as a facilitator who, more than provide instruction, offers proposals according to participants' needs; (3) given that participants have a certain previous experience, it must be connected to new contents and knowledge; and (4) learning must be connected to social responsibility (Vallejo-Romo, 2015).

Andragogy seeks to train people capable of self-management and multidisciplinary work, it also promotes flexible experiences that are grounded in reality, peer interaction, the appreciation toward previous experiences, and of methods adapted to adults' conditions. Given the perspectives of knowledge society and knowledge economy, the use of ICTs must be considered to provide common learning environments in every training process (Rodríguez-Álvarez, 2011).

4.5 EXPECTED BENEFITS

The benefits of an SPCS model can be noted in the increase in the scientific production and communication indicators of the institution where it is implemented, both in quantity and quality. This is a large benefit, as scientific communication is considered to be among the main assets that define the quality of knowledge institutions.

Scientific production and communication must justify the public investment dedicated to scientific research in any knowledge institution. Currently, the measurement of scientific competitiveness in such institutions is considered to be more important than traditional higher education indicators (student enrollment, amount of professors, number of graduates, among others), because knowledge generation through scientific communication takes precedence over teaching as an exclusive activity.

Governmental visions consider that the development of scientific competitiveness in knowledge institutions allows the following: (1) characterize the quality of scientific research and assess improvements during determined periods of time; (2) identify scientific development, strengths and weaknesses of various disciplines, and lines of research; (3) characterize research activities by institution type; (4) conduct comparative analyses from different perspectives; and (5) analyze and project performance by using the main scientometric indicators (CONICYT, 2014). Scientific communication justifies the existence, permanence, and development of science, it becomes a social phenomenon, a human necessity, and a public service. Scientific development is a fundamental characteristic of developed societies, as it allows reducing their dependence upon other people, institutions, and countries.

REFERENCES

Barone, S. (2009). *Las estructuras organizacionales: Cultura, principios y modelos para la innovación.* Santo Domingo, Dominican Republic: Federación Internacional de Fe y Alegría.

Bates College. (2011). The structure, format, content, and style of a journal-style scientific paper. <http://abacus.bates.edu/~ganderso/biology/resources/writing/HTWsections.html> Accessed 16.08.09.

Bedoya, J. (2003). *Pedagogía. ¿Enseñar a pensar?* Bogota, Colombia: Colombia: ECOE.

Betancourt-López, V. (2003). *La comunicación científica.* La Habana, Cuba: Finalay Ediciones.

Chiroque-Solano, R. (2016). La investigación bibliométrica en el Perú y la importancia de su aplicación. <http://eprints.rclis.org/13246/1/La_investigacion_bibliometrica_en_el_Peru.pdf> Accessed 16.08.09.

CONICYT (2014). *Principales indicadores cienciométricos de la actividad científica chilena: Informe 2014, una mirada a 10 años.* Madrid, Spain; Valparaiso, Chile: Scimago Lab. <http://www.conicyt.cl/informacioncientifica/files/2014/08/Informe-de-Chile-2012.pdf> Accessed 16.08.09.

Corpas-Pastor, G. (2001). La competencia traductora: a propósito del texto médico especializado. In C. Valerio-Garcés, & I. De la Cruz-Babanillas (Eds.), *Traducción y nuevas tecnologías: Herramientas auxiliares del traductor* (pp. 29–46). Alcalá de Henares, Spain: Universidad de Alcalá de Henares.

Fernández-Valdés, M., & Núñez-Paula, I. (2007). Metodología para el estudio de las necesidades de información, conocimiento y aprendizaje en las bibliotecas y centros de documentación de salud. *Acimed, 15*(4), 1–19. <http://scielo.sld.cu/pdf/aci/v15n4/aci04407.pdf> Accessed 16.08.09.

Franco Aixelá, J. (2013). La traducción científico-técnica: Aportaciones desde los estudios de traducción. *Letras, 53,* 37–60. <http://www.revistas.una.ac.cr/index.php/letras/article/view/6316> Accessed 16.08.09.

Freyre, M. (1999). *Textos especializados: Comprensión y traducción por profesionales del área científico-técnico y por traductores.* La Plata, Argentina: Universidad Nacional de La Plata.

Fundación Telefónica (2014). *Innovaciones educativas: Top 100.* Madrid, Spain: Fundación Telefónica. <http://www.fundaciontelefonica.com/educacion_innovacion/desafio_educacion/edicion-2014/las-100-innovaciones> Accessed 16.08.09.

Gendina, N. (2017). Information culture and information literacy as a scientific direction and a field of educational activities in Russia. In D. Sales, & M. Pinto (Eds.), *Pathways into information literacy and communities of practice: Teaching approaches and case studies* (pp. 167–201). Oxford, UK: Chandos Publishing. Available from http://dx.doi.org/10.1016/B978-0-08-100673-3.00007-1.

Giraldo, U., Abad, D., & Díaz, E. (2005). *Bases para una política de calidad de la educación superior en Colombia.* Bogota, Colombia: Consejo Nacional de Acreditación.

Goñi-Camejo, I. (2008). El qué y el cómo del diagnóstico del sistema de información gerencial. *Acimed, 17*(5), 1–19. <http://www.bvs.sld.cu/revistas/aci/v17_5_08/aci04508.htm> Accessed 16.08.09.

Goodwin, L., Kozleski, E., Muth, R., Rhodes, L., & White, K. (2006). Establishing a center to support faculty research. *Innovative Higher Education, 30*(4), 251–268. Available from http://dx.doi.org/10.1007/s10755-005-8347-z.

Gorbea-Portal, S. (2013). Tendencias transdisciplinarias en los estudios métricos de la información y su relación con la gestión de la información y del conocimiento. *Perspectivas em Gestão & Conhecimento, João Pessoa, 3*(1), 13–27. <http://periodicos.ufpb.br/ojs2/index.php/pgc/article/view/14175> Accessed 16.08.09.

Griffies, S., Perrie, W., & Hull, G. (2013). Elements of style for writing scientific journal articles. s.l.: Elsevier. <https://www.publishingcampus.elsevier.com/websites/elsevier_publishingcampus/files/Skills%20training/Elements_of_Style.pdf> Accessed 16.08.09.

Grover, R. (1993). A proposal model for diagnosing information needs. *School Library Media Quarterly, 21*(2), 95–100.

Hernández-Salazar, P. (2011). La importancia de la satisfacción del usuario. *Documentación de las Ciencias de la Información, 34*, 349–368. Available from http://dx.doi.org/10.5209/rev_DCIN.2011.v34.36463.

Hernández-Salazar, P. (2013). El perfil del usuario de la información. *Investigación Bibliotecológica*, 7(15), 16–22. <http://www.revistas.unam.mx/index.php/ibi/article/view/3816> Accessed 16.08.09.

Hintze, J. (2006). Administración de estructuras organizativas. *Transformación: Estado y Democracia, 37*, 67–106. <https://www.onsc.gub.uy/onsc1/images/stories/Publicaciones/RevistaONSC/r37/37-8.pdf> Accessed 16.08.09.

Martínez, L. (2013). *Cómo buscar y usar información científica: Guía para estudiantes universitarios*. Santander, Spain: Universidad de Cantabria.

Martínez-López, A. (2009). Sobre la traducción de documentos médico-legales (de español a inglés): Práctica profesional y explotación didáctica en el aula de traducción especializada. *REDIT, 2*, 33–52.

Martín-Moreno, C. (2007). Metodología de investigación en estudios de usuarios. *Revista General de Información y Documentación, 17*(2), 129–149. <http://revistas.ucm.es/index.php/RGID/article/view/10253> Accessed 16.08.09.

Martín-Sampere, M., & Rey-Rocha, J. (2007). *El papel de los científicos en la comunicación de la ciencia y la tecnología a la sociedad: actitudes, aptitudes e implicación*. Madrid, Spain: Consejo Superior de Investigaciones Científicas.

Maya-Ampudia, C., Ángeles-Zavala, O., & Camarena-Olmedo, J. (2014). Diagnóstico de necesidades de educación continua mediante un método grupal y un método individual. *Investigación en Educación Médica, 3*(12), 177–186. <http://riem.facmed.unam.mx/node/326> Accessed 16.08.09.

Mintzberg, H. (1983). *Structure in fives: Designing effective organizations*. Englewood Cliffs, NJ: Prentice Hall.

Montana, P., & Charnov, B. (1993). *Management: A streamlined course for students and business people*. New York: Barron's Business Review Series.

MSPS (Spain) (2009). *Actualización de guías de práctica clínica en el Sistema Nacional de Salud: manual metodológico*. Madrid, Spain: Ministerio de Ciencia e Innovación.

Pérez-Morfi, D., Núñez-Paula, I., Font-Graupera, E., & Lazcano-Herrera, C. (2013). Diagnóstico de la gestión de información de un centro de investigaciones, utilizando el modelo AMIGA. *Ciencias de la Información, 44*(2), 43–53. <http://www.redalyc.org/articulo.oa?id=181430077005> Accessed 16.08.09.

Ramírez-Martínez, D., Martínez-Ruiz, L., & Castellanos-Domínguez, O. (2012). *Divulgación y difusión del conocimiento: Las revistas científicas*. Bogota, Colombia: Universidad Nacional de Colombia.

Rey-Marín, C. (2000). La satisfacción del usuario: Un concepto en alza. *Anales de Documentación, 3*, 139–153. <http://www.redalyc.org/articulo.oa?id=63500309> Accessed 16.08.09.

Rodríguez-Álvarez, M. (2011). *Modelo andragógico de capacitaciones (texto didáctico)*. (Master thesis). Guatemala: Universidad Panamericana.

Rojas-Betancur, H. (2011). Docencia y formación científica universitaria. *Magis: Revista Internacional de Investigación en Educación*, *4*(7), 121–136. <http://www.redalyc.org/pdf/2810/281021741007.pdf> Accessed 16.08.09.

Torres-Rodríguez, M. (2013). *Propuestas de promoción de la comunicación científica en docentes e investigadores: Caso UACH–Facultad de Filosofía y Letras. (Master thesis)*. Chihuahua, Mexico: Universidad Autónoma de Chihuahua.

United Nations Educational, Scientific and Cultural Organization (2005). *¿Cómo promover el interés por la cultura científica?: Una propuesta didáctica fundada para la educación científica de jóvenes de 15 a 18 años*. Santiago, Chile: United Nations Educational, Scientific and Cultural Organization.

Vallejo-Romo, L. (2015). Características de los programas de capacitación andragógicos y los procesos de aprendizaje para la seguridad minera peruana. *Revista del Instituto de Investigación RIIGEO*, *18*(36), 71–75. <http://revistasinvestigacion.unmsm.edu.pe/index.php/iigeo/article/view/12021> Accessed 16.08.09.

Villaruel-Fuentes, M. (2012). Scientific training and skills development for agricultural research in experimental sciences. *Revista Iberoamericana de las Ciencias Biológicas y Agropecuarias*, *1*(1), 1–25. <http://www.ciba.org.mx/index.php/CIBA/article/view/14/230> Accessed 16.08.09.

CONCLUSION

Higher education and research imply conducting actions that are related to globalization and knowledge generation, which is a characteristic of the knowledge society. Such actions make knowledge institutions the main entities in charge of social development under the knowledge economy's fundamental elements.

Knowledge institutions especially depend on the expectations that governments and societies have placed on them, by considering them as the centers for training new professionals and as engines for the economy through their development of research projects that are related with productive, innovation, and development processes. These processes are conducted for the public good and for society's sake.

Professional training requires constantly updating contents and ways of working, especially for "emerging professions," which acknowledge the presence of traditional disciplines while they also seek to offer efficient solutions for society's problems.

The professions that knowledge institutions develop can have three dimensions: (1) those professions that are highly demanded, which solve immediate social problems and even generate social wellbeing through knowledge generation; (2) professions that indirectly support other scientific disciplines in generating knowledge and research, and support them in conducting scientific communication; and (3) professions that serve as support disciplines and that also can generate research and scientific communication by themselves. Information Science fits within the latter two categories, as it supports research and knowledge generation through knowledge creation, preservation, dissemination, and communication, and it can even contribute to social mobility.

Scientific communication in knowledge institutions adopts diverse perspectives: ideological, functional, structural, and even cultural. However, it needs a starting point that legitimizes it and acknowledges the following: (1) knowledge is recognized as scientific when it is generalizable, trustworthy, and valid; (2) measuring research results and scientific communication requires recording evidences, both quantitative (number of scientific products published) and qualitative (quality levels regarding visibility and impact), which allow determining advances and monitor scientific growth; and (3) the influence of individual and collective work over scientific communication must be measured in the short, medium, and long terms.

Legitimizing scientific production and communication in knowledge institutions as an essential characteristic of their scientific culture, requires that its main stakeholders (especially professors and researchers) acknowledge them as valuable and important elements for personal, institutional, regional, and disciplinary performances. Moreover, they are functions that must be perceived as daily activities that are typical of an academic's profile, although this is not always commonly accepted, because they are considered by some as voluntary activities. If scientific production and communication are not considered important in a given knowledge institution, this paradigm must be changed, as they are necessary for training new professionals with a strong scientific culture. Any knowledge institution must clearly establish its scientific function within its structure, acknowledging its importance, promoting it, and planning strategies and initiatives to ensure its development. This will be key in order to develop the scientific culture of any institution.

Information professionals' engagement in scientific production and communication can represent an innovative trend within their professional exercise, it also demands them to develop especial competences and an awareness of how to harness and strengthen diverse available aspects, such as: technological infrastructure, the adoption of adequate methodological approaches for scientific work, seeking to apply added value to the actions developed, formulating knowledge products, and developing continuing education experiences. This results in imagining information professionals capable of contributing to the development of the scientific culture and scientific competitiveness of their institutions.

The development of a profession must be clear and be based upon constant change and paradigm shifts. This must emerge from the profession itself and from its stakeholders. In the case of information professionals, it is necessary to include training about scientific production and communication in their curricula. In their working lives, they must identify the elements in which they can innovate regarding the services they offer to knowledge institutions and specialized users.

INDEX

Note: Page numbers followed by "*f*" and "*t*" refer to figures and tables.

F

G

H

I

K

Made in the USA
Monee, IL
13 September 2026

62977001R00085